The

PUZZLE

Of

WATERGATE

WHY WATERGATE?

The big secret WHY behind the 1972 break-in at

the Watergate offices of the Democrat National

Headquarters finally revealed

JEAN ELLEN WILSON

CONTENTS

DEDICATION BY SUBJECT OF THIS BOOK

ALFRED BALDWIN

This book is dedicated to my mentor and best friend, Attorney Robert C. Mirto of West Haven, Connecticut. From our first few days of law school and the subsequent adventures and experience we shared, ours has been a journey through time and history. His outstanding legal ability has been displayed many times in the federal and local courtrooms not only in Connecticut but also on the national scene. Probably his finest hours took place during his representation for me at the various proceedings during the Watergate trial and subsequent congressional hearings. The Watergate matter did not consume months, it consumed years and Robert was always there for me. If there was cement to the bond of friendship, it was Watergate. Thank you for bringing true meaning to the word "friendship."

FOREWORD

Before "watergate" became "Watergate," it was a word meaning "A gate for halting or controlling the flow of water in a watercourse; floodgate." When considered from a certain point of view, the old use is appropriate as a metaphor for "Watergate" as political scandal. That view is that the mighty course of information flowing from those events was indeed controlled by a formidable gate of intrigue.

The recorded history of Watergate is a voluminous sea of truth shot with lies, theories, excuses, fabrications, thwarted ambition, hubris, limelight-grabbing, fear, shame, and paranoia. Participants, major and minor, have contributed their stories limited by viewpoint and distorted by a natural instinct to choose the best of available proofs with character blemishes photoshopped.

But in following the basic formula of telling a tale—who, what, when, where, how, and why—the why has never been satisfactorily answered in any of the accounts. In solving any mystery, motive is paramount, but the real motive for the break-in that made the first cut into the body of the misuse of power has eluded investigators.

Even the culprits wonder about the "why." Why the break-in?

In prison, Colson and Dean confronted Magruder with the question—Why? Why did you order it? Magruder could not answer.

Fifteen years after the break-in when H. R. Haldeman was questioned as to why, he said he'd always wondered himself.

After Ehrlichman had served his sentence, he and his wife ran into James McCord in an airport. Mrs. Ehrlichman, in that aggressive manner typical of wronged political wives, confronted McCord—"Why? Why did you do it?" McCord had no answer.

Of course, there have been many proposed answers to the question: Political research of the opposition. To expose the ties between Larry O'Brien and Howard Hughes. To prove prostitutes were being pimped out of Democratic National Headquarters. To make sure none of those working girls could be linked to White House VIPs. To look for evidence of Nixon's connection to CIA's attempts to assassinate Castro. To discover what other dirt the Democrats had to spring on Nixon in the upcoming presidential campaign. To film the donor lists hoping to find Castro and/or North Korea giving money to the Dems. To delve into the files of the Vietnam Veterans Against the War who allegedly had a desk in the Watergate headquarters.

There were good reasons to discount all the theories put forward. In pursuit of the definitive "why break in," Alfred Baldwin offers up the analogy of a jigsaw puzzle. He has taken pieces of the puzzle of Watergate from his memory and laid them out on the table that is this book. He puts the first piece of the puzzle down and it is just an isolated peculiarity. He adds a second piece and we are looking at a byte of circumstantial evidence. As he joins other pieces where they fit, inexplicable shapes of evidence become part of a discernible whole.

Alfred Baldwin, at the end of his life, has decided to answer the question "Why?"

Al has been battling cancer since 1998 when he underwent a radical prostatectomy that failed to remove all the virulent cells. In 2018, after three additional cancers, he was advised that he was terminal.

In view of this diagnosis coupled with the death of James McCord, Al has made the decision to publish this book.

An underlying question to why Watergate is why Alfred Baldwin. Why did James McCord choose Al Baldwin as his assistant that chaotic spring of 1972? Why reach out to Baldwin, an ex-FBI agent at that time working in academia in New Haven, Connecticut, when there was a plethora of ex-FBI in the Washington area?

To get some idea of what that criteria was, we need to look at Baldwin's life.

In the massive archive of Watergate material, Alfred C. Baldwin III, the man who monitored the telephone bug at Democratic Headquarters and acted as watchman the night of the break-in, is given short shrift. He goes unmentioned by Woodward and Bernstein. Jim Hougan, author of *Secret Agenda,* described Baldwin as a wisecracking bachelor who was so engrossed in watching *The Attack of the Puppet People* on TV that he failed to warn the Watergate burglars the police had arrived. Martha Mitchell judged Baldwin to be "the gauchest character I've ever met." In John Sirica's memoir, *To Set the Record Straight*, the judge seemed to be of the opinion that Baldwin was either a fool or a liar because he could not remember the name of the guard to whom he delivered a package. E. Howard Hunt accused him of being a double agent. (When James McCord testified before the Senate Watergate Committee, the first question he was asked was "Was Alfred Baldwin a double agent?") Baldwin is not listed in the index in Leon Jaworski's *The Right and the Power* while the authors of *Silent Coup* present Baldwin as if he had a walk-on part in a play. Baldwin is not listed in the index to G. Gordon Liddy's book *Will*, because Liddy refers to him only as McCord's assistant.

But, on the contrary, Baldwin's background, character, education, and experience make him a substantial witness testifying as to heretofore untold information within the arc of events known as Watergate. Most importantly, rather, his story contains the key to the great mystery of Watergate—the *why* of the break-in.

In all of the hue and cry of multiple investigations, the mob of press, bureaucrats, anti-war activists, and government opponents in pursuit of the demonized Nixon, Baldwin was dismissed as a minor actor, even flunkey, in the drama of Watergate.

He was much more than that.

Al Baldwin believes that he was recruited by McCord on the basis of a psychological profile put together by the CIA. In the '70s, there was a special section within the agency experimenting with extrasensory perception and other mind-bending possibilities. Psychological profiling was a standard intelligence tool. Cold War VIPs were routinely profiled. It is claimed that one of the main duties of Howard Hunt's position as one of the Plumbers was to send documents by and about White House personnel to Langley to be mined by the profilers.

To get an idea of what might have been considered in a Baldwin profile, let's look at his family background and a few highlights of his life and career before Watergate.

1

THRESHOLD YEARS

H e was born on June 23, 1936, in New Haven, Connecticut, the second of twins to Alfred Carlton Baldwin II and Veronica (Vera) Traub Baldwin. His father's family was English and Protestant, his mother's German and Catholic.

His paternal grandmother was a Clemons, a sister to Samuel Clemons who wrote as Mark Twain. His paternal great-uncle was Raymond Baldwin who had the distinction of being the only man in Connecticut history who held the three positions of governor, U.S. senator, and State Supreme Court justice. However, Al Baldwin never touted his prominent kinsman's name as there had been a rift between that branch of the family and his own, the cause of which his father never revealed. His grandfather Baldwin had no formal education but worked in a factory at night and a law office in the daytime. On the latter job, he learned the law and, eventually, became a Supreme Court judge with the character of a venerable Connecticut Yankee. One of his cousins was Victor Clarke, a prominent officer in the

Connecticut State Police, and Clarke would play a significant role in a trau-matic event that occurred in young Al's childhood as related hereinafter.

His mother, Veronica, had nine siblings. She and one sister were the only two born in the United States. Al's maternal grandfather, Adolph Traub, brought his family out of Germany in the 1890s, anxious to avoid service in the Kaiser's war. Adolph's machinist skills made New Haven, already a thriving industrial center, a good choice to settle his family. In World War II, the location became a hub of corporations like Pratt & Whitney, Winchester Arms, and Sikorsky producing armaments, aircraft, and other war materials.

Al's father, Alfred Baldwin II, his father's brother Ralph, and his father's sister, Harriet, never attended a formal K through 12 school but were homeschooled. Baldwin II passed the competitive examination for West Point and entered the United States Military Academy; Ralph passed the competitive examination for Annapolis and entered the United States Naval Academy. Alfred II served in the artillery branch of the Army in World War I. He was wounded in France when his horse-drawn caisson was blown up while moving to a new firing position. After hospitaliza-tion in France, he was shipped back to the United States where he was discharged due to his wounds. Ralph, after graduating from Annapolis, had a thirty-year career in the Navy. He was so severely wounded in the World War II Battle of Leyte Gulf in the Pacific that he spent almost a year in Bethesda Hospital and the rest of his life paralyzed on his right side. Al III said that Army–Navy games were the occasion of lively competition between his father and uncle when he was a boy.

Baldwin II, barred from an Army career by his wounds, entered George Washington University Law School, completing what should have been a three-year course in one year.

Baldwin III wondered about the influence of his formidable family on his character. "What makes a man?" he once mused. "What basic causes set a man on a certain path when he begins his life's journey? Is it his color? Is it his religion? His schooling? His time in the military? His family? What forms the spirit and soul that becomes a man's personality and character?"

His father's character was forged in homeschooling and West Point, and his creed was "honor, duty, country." His father despised a liar. It was as if all evil began with a lie. That the peril of lying was the gravest of sins was a lesson learned early on by the Baldwin twins. Al declared: "That stuck with me my entire life. It's important to me when I'm dealing with somebody that they're being truthful. If I find somebody's lying to me, I lose respect. I may not say anything, but I then avoid that individual."

Puzzled by the many stories the loquacious Al Baldwin III told of various exploits when he used an alias or worked undercover living a lie or pretending to have evidence against a suspect he was interrogating, I asked how he could justify these untruths while holding to such a strict principle of truthfulness. He was vague in his answer but the gist of it was that lying was excused in the line of work. In light of some of the behavior I observed over the six months of taping Baldwin, I am not so sure that, in practice, the line between work and the other facets of his life could always be steadfast.

Alfred and his sister, Veronica (Ronnie) Baldwin, entered grammar school at the age of four in 1940. They lived in rural North Haven, a farming community adjacent to Hamden. St. Boniface in New Haven, the German Catholic school which they attended, was bookended by the Polish Catholic St. Stanislaus and the Italian Catholic St. Anthony. Whether young Al and his sister went north or south to and from the bus stop, they had to run the gauntlet of bullying by Polish or Italian youngsters. The 1940s were the years of World War II in Europe and even children had nationalist loyalties.

Back of the house occupied by the family in the 1940s was a cow barn that was important to the Baldwins. The young Baldwin twins spent time in its loft pretending it was a war room where they planned battles played out in the trenches they dug around the building. During these years and for many years after, Vera Baldwin supplemented her husband's income by collecting antiques at flea markets and estate sales, storing them in this barn until she could sell them at a profit. Her two brothers would help move large items.

All the Traub siblings came together to improve the beach property at New Haven's Silver Sands purchased at an affordable price after a 1936 hurricane had devastated all the rest of the buildings on the nearby shoreline. What had been a hot dog stand eventually became a beach cottage with five bedrooms upstairs, living room with fireplace, and kitchen and dining area that accommodated twelve to sixteen. The Traub/Baldwin tribes spent many weekends at the cottage, always improving the beachfront residence.

One of the favorite pastimes in that more tech-free innocent time was dragging a huge horseshoe crab on invisible fishing line from the water across the beach, frightening those who came across its path while the onlookers on the porch of the cottage laughed hilariously.

So young Alfred C. Baldwin III, "Al," grew up among a close-knit unit of family support who worked together and played together.

In this atmosphere, Al also learned the discipline of work. He and his cousins, between the volleyball and softball games at the beach, acted as the maintenance crew for the communal summer house. In the winter, he delivered papers and groceries on his bicycle. In his early teens, his father, counselor for a local cinder block factory, secured for him the job of sweeping out the debris left in the kilns after the blocks were baked. Al said, "This was my father's way of saying you learn to be a man by working and it instilled in me a work ethic that remained throughout my life and I owe him gratitude for that."

The Great Depression had made Baldwin II a believer in government service. The pay, at that time, was less than that offered by private enterprise, but the job security and benefits were more important to him after that perilous economic experience. He abandoned his career as a private attorney and became an unemployment commissioner for the state of Connecticut. An unemployment commissioner is a quasi-judge who hears unemployment claim cases and renders decisions.

Alfred III entered Notre Dame all-male high school in West Haven, Connecticut, in 1948. In the summer of his senior year, his father suffered major injuries in an automobile accident and was hospitalized in St. Francis Hospital in Hartford, Connecticut, for an extensive stay. The possibility loomed that the senior Baldwin would never return to work.

Although his father was urging him toward either West Point or Annapolis, the senior Baldwin's perilous health influenced Al to continue his education near home. He chose to attend Fairfield University in Fairfield, Connecticut, run by the Jesuits.

In casting about for a career plan, Al did take a Naval Aviation test. Having met all the requirements for acceptance to the Naval Aviation program, the final test was to be given at the Naval Hospital in Albany, New York. It would consist of a complete physical examination. The eye exam portion revealed Al lacked depth perception, a flaw he attributed to a severe eye injury experienced at the age of three.

Al's German shepherd was in the Baldwin backyard when a neighbor's Doberman Pinscher suddenly appeared and fell upon the boy's puppy.

Al ran out to save the pup and the Doberman turned on the toddler, biting him on the left side of his head in the area of his left eye.

Fortunately, Victor Clarke, a kinsman and a Connecticut State trooper lieutenant, was then at the Baldwin house on a visit. He forced the attacking dog away from the boy and turned his attention to Al's severe wounds. After administering basic first aid, Clarke and Al's mother rushed the boy to the family doctor's house in which his medical office was located. (In those days there was no hospital emergency room.)

The injury inflicted by the Doberman was so severe that hope of recovery of eyesight meant having the eyes of three-year-old Al bandaged for four months. Overcoming this period of temporary blindness, which surely seemed very long to a small child and was very difficult for an active boy, was the first character-building experience of Al Baldwin's life and one that prohibited an aviation career.

(The incident did not prevent Baldwin from being a dog-lover. When illness made it imperative that he put down his two canine companions, it was one of the worst days of his life.)

Al never played either high school or college sports, but he had a friend who was a football hero and went into the Marines during the Korean War. Al was so impressed when he came home in his resplendent uniform that he determined to join that service. Having started school at such a young age, he was too young to join, but at the end of his first year at Fairfield, he was accepted into a newly initiated program, Platoon Leaders Course, which allowed one to be eligible to become a Marine officer upon graduation.

2

THE CHALLENGE –
THE UNITED STATES MARINE CORPS

During his sophomore, junior, and senior years at Fairfield University, Al Baldwin was an enlisted member of the United States Marine Corps Reserve. His summer months were spent at Marine Corps training facilities preparing him for his commissioning as a Marine officer.

In 1957, Baldwin became the first graduate of Fairfield University to complete the Platoon Leaders Course program, thereby becoming a 2nd Lieutenant in the Marine Corps. After training stints at Camp Lejeune, North Carolina, and at the U.S. Marine Corps Base at Quantico, Virginia, he was stationed at the latter facility which consisted of the basic school for Marine officers, special schools for senior military officers from different branches, and a war college for foreign officers. Also, at Quantico was the Federal Bureau of Investigation's (FBI's) training academy, an adjunct to the FBI headquarters in Washington used in weapons/firearms and other training for which the facility was adapted.

The Marine unit to which Al was assigned was the on-base officer corps which complemented and supported all the schools that existed. The officers that were assigned to Mainside wore many different hats. One did not have just one specific job.

One of the most interesting of Al's assignments was as the officer in charge of the boat facilities at Quantico and of the stables occupied by a group of horses that belonged to the commanding general, General Victor Krulak. The general stood about five/four and had a love of horses and polo, and one part of Al's charge was to make sure that the general's horses were kept in top shape. (His son, Charles C. Krulak, became the 31st Commandant of the Marine Corps on July 1, 1995.)

One day Al received a call from his gunnery sergeant at the stables that the horses were to be loaded on a World War II LCVP boat and transported across the Potomac. Would Al care to watch the operation? Of course, he would. At the boatyard, Al watched with interest as the boat which had just come out of dry dock began to move across the river. The scene became even more interesting as, about halfway across, the boat slowly began to sink. Al stood on the riverbank and watched with consternation as the two horses aboard began to swim in opposite directions. There was nothing Al could do but observe the boat crew try, but fail, to corral the polo steeds in one direction. In fact, one swam to the opposite shore as the other swam back to our side. Still, it was only through the heroic efforts of the enlisted men in the crew that the horses were returned to the stables safe and without injury.

It was discovered that the sea plug of the LCVP had not been replaced, an extremely amateur error.

Those involved in the disaster attempted to delete the incident from history but General Krulak found out and, of course, Al was the one in charge, so he was instructed to report to the general's headquarters. Al related that this was the most frightful day he suffered in the Marine Corps—to face General Krulak and his wrath.

Baldwin found the general stalking up and down the length of his office. He was on the receiving end of a twenty-minute tirade before Krulak sat down behind his desk, pinned his very junior officer with a stare, and barked, "What have you got to say for yourself to save your butt?" Al looked at the general, thinking of his father's mantra, of honor, duty, and country, and with the memory of his father's admonishing voice saying "God help you if you step one inch out of line with any kind of story that doesn't stick to the facts," could only offer, "General, there is nothing I can say." Al believes his refraining from excuses or buck-passing surprised Krulak for that worthy man was silent for a long moment before saying: "I intended to reduce you in rank, but I am going to confine you to quarters for thirty days—and I mean confine."

Well, strict confinement did not hold. An unusually severe snowstorm hit Virginia and officers—including Al—could not resist the temptation to use sleds on the hills of Quantico. Baldwin remembers that, at the end of thirty days, he was summoned by General Krulak who wanted to know if he had anything further to add to the official report of the incident. Al said, "No, Sir," and decades later said, "Thank goodness he did not ask me if I had been faithful to the sentence of confinement for I would have had to confess to sledding."

An escapade pattern of that time at the Quantico base was the Great Rabbit Hunts. About once a month after Happy Hour, Al and some of his fellow officers would get into their Volkswagens and sporty convertibles and depart for the Marine Corps golf course where President Eisenhower loved to play the game. The fairway adjacent to the bachelor officers' quarters was home to hundreds of rabbits which the happily inebriated officers endeavored to catch with fishing nets in the course of which they tore up that section of the course. This forced the ground crew to keep stacks of sod with which to repair the ground on Saturday morning before the generals and other VIPs teed off. The MPs did everything in their power to catch the vandals who were doing this damage but failed, perhaps because a certain captain in charge of the force and his adjutant, a certain lieutenant, never found that there was enough evidence to prosecute.

At Quantico, Al Baldwin forged a friendship with a man who proved to be a positive influence on his career—Special Agent Henry "Hank" Sloan who was then Director of the FBI school at Quantico. Among other resources under his control was the firearm section.

Al met Sloan when he went on a tour of the FBI facilities under Sloan's control. After the inspection, Al invited the agent to come to Happy Hour at the Officer's Club and he showed up one Friday.

The two became friends and one day in conversation Al learned that for some time Sloan had been asking for assistance with a problem he had with the grounds around the FBI building there at Quantico. It so happened that Al's roommate, Rodney Fulton, was in charge of the maintenance department. Of course, upon being petitioned by Baldwin, Fulton took care of the problem with alacrity and the result was that "Hank" Sloan offered his support as a reference if Al was ever interested in becoming an FBI agent.

3

UPGRADE CHALLENGE AND PRESTIGIOUS EMPLOYMENT: LAW SCHOOL AND THE FEDERAL BUREAU OF INVESTIGATION

The senior Baldwin's health continued to deteriorate. Gangrene set in around the metal pin in his leg, forcing amputation. Al went home every weekend he could, and the situation there troubled his strong sense of duty. After some time, he made the decision to leave the Marine Corps when his term was over with the intention of eventually joining the FBI. At that time, one had to have a law or accounting degree, fluency in a language, or electronic/technical capability needed by the nation's investigative force to become an FBI agent. Al determined that he would go back home, help with his father's care, and attend law school. This he did.

He was accepted by the University of Connecticut Law School, Hartford, Connecticut, in the class that was to graduate in 1963. He was in school or working part-time in the day and caring for his father, who was getting progressively worse, at night. This allowed his mother to work her late shift at Pratt & Whitney Aircraft in East Hartford, Connecticut.

Alfred Baldwin II's service as an unemployment commissioner became impossible when, as a result of his injuries, he lost his voice. As noted, a commissioner was a type of judge, deciding whether the state or a private company owed a worker pay, and a judge was required to speak. Baldwin II did not have enough years in office to be eligible for retirement. However, he was so highly regarded that Abe Ribicoff, Connecticut's governor, went out of his way to see to it that a special bill was unanimously passed by the legislature giving Al's father full retirement benefits.

After three years of law school, Al was accepted as a candidate for the FBI and was scheduled to begin training with the class of June 1963. Because of this commitment, Al was allowed to take his final exams ahead of the class. On learning that he had passed all of the required tests, Al immediately went to the hospital to give his proud father the news that his son now had a law degree. After visiting a while, he set out for home, traveling a local road south from Hartford, Connecticut to Hamden, Connecticut. Enroute, he noted a state police car headed in the opposite direction and thought he glimpsed a woman in the passenger seat. On arriving home, he found a note from his mother on the kitchen table. His father had died shortly after his son's visit.

The FBI allowed Al to reschedule and his new training class began in July of 1963. After burying his father, he had time to prepare for his move to Washington, D.C. Arriving in the capital, he checked in at FBI Headquarters which was then in its old location on Pennsylvania Avenue, a site shared with the United States attorney's office. There he enquired about housing arrangements only to be told he was on his own. He made his way to a bar called the Rocket Room which he had discovered in his Marine days. The bar, located at 1108 New York Avenue across the street from the Greyhound bus station, was co-owned by Gunny Sergeant Roth, who was called "Dutch" by his friends.

Dutch was a legend in the Corps. When Baldwin sighted him at Quantico, Dutch was overweight, and he went about the base without "cover," (in Marine lingo without his hat), and, against all rules, with his top button unfastened and his tie pulled away from his neck. Although this carelessness was totally unacceptable in the Corps, for some reason Dutch got away with it.

Al learned why no officer ever challenged Dutch on his cavalier dress code. One day when the commandant of the Marines, General David M. Shoup, was at Quantico to speak at the graduation of a group of Korean officers, Al watched as Dutch walked across the compound to wrap Shoup in a bearhug. "I just stood there," said Al, "thinking My God, this man has more guts than I will ever have." He later learned that their relationship went back to World War II and a Pacific island where Dutch saved the life of a young officer who was to become the recipient of a Medal of Honor and subsequently the 22nd Commandant of the Corps. Legend has it that a young, trim Marine Sergeant Roth had something to do with Shoup's medal.

Dutch was behind the bar when Al arrived at the Rocket Room. After a hearty reunion, Al asked Dutch if he knew of any apartments available in the D.C. area. Dutch leaned across the bar and pointed to a man sitting at the bar opposite Al. "He is a Naval aviator and is attending some government school here in Washington," said Dutch. "He told me if I ever revealed what school it was, he'd have to kill me. He also told me he might be looking for a roommate so I'll introduce you." He did so. The man was Lieutenant Commander Jack Bell, U.S. Navy, and he and Al became roommates and good friends. He was in training with the CIA in preparation for a posting at an embassy in North Africa. For the next three months, on the odd weekend, the two would go to an airport in search of stewardess dates, a quest almost always ending in success. Jack also accompanied Al to Connecticut where Al's family and friends gave him a warm welcome. Sadly, Jack disappeared while on a photographic mission over North Africa.

While in FBI training, Al spent a good many hours with Dutch at the Rocket Room and through him met Senator Tom Dodd of Connecticut who was a silent partner in the enterprise. (Dodd's son Chris also joined the exclusive club that was the Senate of the United States.) The elder Dodd was a former FBI agent, and he encouraged Al to call on him if there was ever anything he could do for him.

Al remembers his FBI training vividly. The postponement necessitated by his father's death put him in a group largely made up of government employees rather than civilian attorneys and accountants. In fact, most of his fellow trainees had special skills in fingerprinting, crime analysis, and other fields that supported investigations. Since prospective FBI agents were by their nature of selection more educated than the average citizen, the training had to be above average. And in Al's judgment the challenges of the curriculum were extraordinary.

Al had stumbled over the preliminaries leading up to acceptance. The first time was when he failed a section of the examination dealing with word association. Instead of ruling him out, Frank Johnson, the agent who was processing his application, handed him a stack of some fifteen issues of *Readers Digest* and directed him to go home, study the "Word Power" feature in each one and come back in two weeks to take again the section he had failed. This Al did and aced on the second try.

Another hurdle to acceptance was Al's answer to the question, "Do you have a relative who is or has been a United States senator or Member of Congress?" Since Al had never used his famous great uncle, Raymond Baldwin, as a reference, he answered "No." The FBI took exception to what they considered an untruth. Al explained that the man might be a blood relative, but he had learned at a young age that due to the family split he was, when asked if he were kin to Raymond Baldwin, to say "No." Actually Al had met his great-uncle only once. The renowned jurist came to the University of Connecticut to deliver a speech and, to the surprise of the dean of the law school, and to Al, asked if he might speak with his kinsman then attending the law school. The judge and his law student great-nephew had a short, polite exchange in the dean's office.

These two hiccups overcome, Al apprised Hank Sloan that he had been accepted as a candidate and Sloan had given him some pointers. "One—I want you to be extremely alert to what happens in the first hour of training. Be observant and make a mental note of everything you see. Two—when you go into a men's room be sure there is no one else in a stall before you share anything confidential."

The first hour of training arrived. The would-be agents were seated alphabetically, giving Al the third seat at the front. The agent who was in charge of the July 1963 class spoke of the guidelines and was droning on about housekeeping details and contact numbers when a man in shabby street clothes burst into the room followed by two men in suits who captured the man and threw him to the ground. The "culprit" was handcuffed, and the threesome exited the classroom. "Now," said the man conducting the class, "there are blue books under your seats. Write down everything you have just seen in your blue book including as much detail as you can recall." Al remembered years later, "My eyes went skyward and I said a silent thank you to Hank Sloan." Al received a high grade and a "well done" for his report.

Al's second mentor was Julian Clark, the FBI's firearms instructor, whom Al also met at Quantico.

Clark often joined Baldwin for Happy Hour at the Officer's Club. The Marine speculated that his friend came for the highly rated food for which the Club was known rather than the Liar's Poker they played.

Julian Clark was a marksman without equal. He could do things with a machine gun or a handgun that just did not seem humanly possible. He could shoot accurately over his shoulder, under his arms, through his legs; he could cut a playing card's horizontal edge. He started hunting game in his native North Carolina when he was a small boy. Al admired him and took every opportunity to go out to the FBI range and shoot with his hero. Although he never even came close to matching his scores, the exercises allowed Baldwin to learn how to handle and to fire a weapon and that ability helped him to become an agent.

Julian gave Al a hint about another surprise test that presented during his FBI training tenure. This occurred at the FBI's Hogan's Alley at the Quantico FBI campus. Hogan's Alley is a row of buildings used in presenting scenarios an agent might have to face. "You will," Julian told Al, "be ordered to make an arrest that will be physically impossible for you to do, so you will have to think out of the box to master the situation."

In the latter phase of training, the future agents spent time on the Quantico gun range practicing firing from 30 yards, 50 yards, 100 yards with live ammunition. Early on each one had been issued a red tip 38. These guns had been rendered inoperable and did not fire. Student agents wore them in holsters, took them home to practice drawing and handling techniques. In self-defense exercises, the future agents learned cautionary moves to prevent a suspect from taking his weapon.

One of those stories handed down from class to class involved an agent in training who happened to be in a Washington bank and used his red tip to capture the perpetrators of an attempted robbery.

Al recounted the challenge about which Clark had warned him:

A day came when we were told an important practice session would take place. Again, because my name began with a "B," I was one of the first to take part in the exercise. I was assigned the role of arrest agent with one assistant. We had to enter an establishment and accomplish an arrest.

We entered the room that was set up like a movie scene in a bar. There were patrons seated at the bar and at tables. They were pointing and saying "He did it. It was him," and there were two bodies on the floor. Standing at the bar was a huge man, close to seven feet tall maybe 289 pounds. (Al learned later he was a special agent and a former Baltimore Colts football player.)

This man, acting the role of an oversized criminal, turned to me and said, "Yeah—I did it so what in the hell are you going to do about it?" I quickly took out my red tip revolver and shot him. Not to kill but to wound. The instructors evinced great surprise. I said, "I just shot this guy—shouldn't he be on the ground?" The suspect looked to the instructors for guidance, one of them nodded and he sank to the floor. I had to borrow another set of handcuffs to put together with his own in order to cuff the guy. Then I turned to an instructor and said, "I think we need an ambulance." The instructors went out the door, and in a few minutes came back in to say only, "Thank you, Mr. Baldwin."

The exercises at Quantico occurred during the final weeks of training and then the candidate agents went back to Washington for written exams. For those who pass, there is a ceremony in which the fledgling agents meet the Honorable J. Edgar Hoover.

Al Baldwin described his own experience which added to his growing awareness of the mythological power of Mr. Hoover and how and why every FBI agent of that era was wary of their leader.

My graduation from the FBI Academy was an event that is embedded in my brain forever because one of the strangest things happened that dramatized how Mr. Hoover's conceits determined an agent's fate.

We were all lined up for the ceremony in the hallway outside Mr. Hoover's office which was huge with sort of an open foyer as a reception area. We had been drilled as to how we were required to behave. Most importantly, when you go into Mr. Hoover's office you must not look down—ever. If you look down, you are gone. I found out in subsequent years that the reason for this prohibition was that Mr. Hoover is very short in stature and never wanted anybody to stand higher than him, so he always stood on a special wooden box so that he was never shorter than anyone else in the room.

Once Mr. Hoover is in the office and he's ready to receive the graduates, alphabetically, one by one, you approach.

So, we go in, and I'm at the very beginning of the line because of my alphabetical position, and after I received my credentials and my badge, Mr. Hoover handed me my 38 revolver and separately, the ammunition for it. You are under instructions not to load that weapon until you get out of the immediate vicinity of Washington, D.C. This is to avoid some new agent misfiring or causing an incident. I don't remember whether it was Mr. Hoover or Mr. Tolson, but somebody shook my hand. And then, according to directions, I moved over to a certain area and stood there as there was to be a group photograph taken of the class with Mr. Hoover. So, the majority of us were standing there until there were only two gentlemen at the end of the line who had Polish names. I don't remember the names, but both began with W, maybe one was Wa and one was Wr. Somehow these two men got reversed in the line so the first gentleman who was supposed to be Wa was Wr. Hoover called his name. The would-be agent replied, "No, sir. I'm so and so." At that point Mr. Tolson attempted to hand the FBI chief the correct credentials. Hoover refused to take them. Rather, he uttered an emphatic "No," and pointed commandingly toward the door. A seasoned agent, who was in the room, came forward and escorted the two gentlemen with Polish names out of the office. To this day, I don't know what happened to those two men, but all of us assumed that they were both gone and that's an example of the deadly capriciousness with which Hoover ruled.

When you're in the field and get to know other agents, and you would relate that story and he'd relate his and that built this—I don't know—what you want to call it—myth of Hoover that was so feared. We knew the other part of his agenda was to strike fear in the hearts of Congressmen and Senators or anyone of position in government with his files of information on every single one of those people. Mr. Hoover could go to Congress and ask for a certain sum of money, and he always left with more money than he asked for because they would gush, 'Oh, you're doing such a wonderful job, we've got to give you a bonus."

Another way he ruled his agents by terror was through instances of arbitrary termination. An agent could be fired on petty grounds like taking too long a lunch hour. It wasn't only losing the job that the lawman had to fear; it was looking for another job without the reference of having been a satisfactory agent that was frightening.

There was a young man, an attorney, whose father owned Union Pacific Railroad and so you know he was a man of political stature and extremely wealthy, and his son, I'm not sure if he was on an unauthorized coffee break or what the circumstances were, but his son was fired from the FBI with prejudice. "Fired with prejudice" on your resume with no details as to why meant that you are going to run into some very serious difficulties when it comes to seeking employment. The human resources person wants to know what "with prejudice" means and contact with the Bureau would only result in "it's just that—with prejudice," and you'll probably never get the job.

Again, this was just another way an unhealthy awe of J. Edgar spread throughout the Bureau plus there was Mark Felt and his crew. Felt was head of a special unit that would come into a field office unannounced and they were like inspector generals. They would come in and go through office files; they reviewed procedures; they went through the time sheets. We didn't have a time clock; we had a sign-in sheet in every office. We were required to "volunteer" hours every day so that Mr. Hoover could go to Congress and testify "every agent in my FBI has worked an average of four hours a day without pay over their required time." So what was an eight to four or nine to five job, you might work from six in the morning 'til seven at night or you came in on a Saturday or a Sunday, but you had to put in what was called Volunteer Overtime (VOT) hours and those hours better be on the time sheets when they were sent to Washington.

We were so psychologically whiplashed, we worked nervously under these conditions without voicing complaint. If it ever crossed your mind that there was some sort of relationship between the venerated director of the Federal Bureau of Investigation (FBI) and his right-hand man, you would squelch it immediately for you would think, God Almighty, somehow they'll read my mind and I'll be fired. At the same time, you lived in dread you would be suspected of homosexuality. Hank Sloan had warned me never make a habit of going into a men's room with another agent. He said, "They're watching you every minute and if they think there is something going on between you and that agent, they're going to be on you like fleas on a hound dog and you may not have done anything but they'll get you to admit any-thing they want you to admit to after several days of interrogation and your job is always on the line."

Upon graduating from the Academy, the Memphis, Tennessee FBI office was Baldwin's first assignment. He arrived there in either late September or early October of 1963 anticipating a posting of a year, the normal duration of a first assignment when a new agent is learning and basically on probation.

Geographically close, the Memphis office was involved in the after-math of the Kennedy assassination in November 1963. Men and equip-ment were sent south to the Dallas area.

Baldwin was partnered with another new agent, Neil Shea, a for-mer New York City detective, and an exceptionally good-looking man who was dating a former girlfriend of Elvis Presley's. Shea was sent to Irvine just outside Dallas. Baldwin was disappointed at not going south with his friend, but he did deliver equipment to support the investigation of the president's assassination.

Because of the suspicion that the CIA is conspiratorial, Mr. Baldwin's belief that in the assassination of President John F. Kennedy, Lee Harvey Oswald was "set up" begs relevancy.

Baldwin believes that the government had Oswald and wanted it to be Oswald. This objective carried through to the Warren Commission which stayed within certain perameters and did not go outside. They knew exactly what they wanted to hear and that's what they were going to hear.

For example, Baldwin cites the shooting of the police officer allegedly by Oswald. When he was arrested inside the theater, Oswald was carrying a 32-caliber gun, yet the police officer was killed by a 38-caliber. Neither weapon will take the other's ammo. The ballistic expert who testified before the Warren Commission was questioned to the point of the discrepancy of caliber when the Chief Justice called for the lunch recess. The expert was not brought back for further questioning when the Commission reassembled.

On that fateful day in Dallas, the route of the president's motorcade was changed. The change offered shooters, especially if one was in the sewer, a better shot. Who authorized the change and why?

There was a large tree between Oswald and the president's car which allowed only a few seconds to take the shot. Granted that he was a good shot, but was he that good with an Italian rifle not known for accuracy?

The shot that killed Kennedy was a frontal shot. The evidence for that is that his head went back, and the back of his skull was blown off.

Returning to Alfred Baldwin's career, he talks about his stint in Tennessee:

Of course, there were agents who took chances in defiance of the atmosphere of fear. For example, I and others would contrive to be out of the office in the last hours before our shift was to end because you risked being chosen as case agent for any Federal criminal investigation occurring in those final business hours. You're at your desk and the Special Agent in Charge (SAC) or the Assistant Special Agent in Charge (ASAC) might come out of his office and look around and you're sitting there. So, he points and says, "Al, we've just had a bank robbery, you're in charge, it's your case, get on it."

Well, Memphis had, at various locations, indoor golf courses similar to those outdoor miniature golf courses with obstacles to which you take children. So you pick one of those putting courses not anywhere near the office and you park your car maybe a block or two away and you go up to spend an hour or two, and the ironic thing is you'd go in and sure enough there would be other agents there with the same marking-time purpose as you, and you'd end up having a team contest.

One day, I was going to waste an hour on one of these golf spots. I parked across the street from a store like a Dollar Store and decided I would pick up a few articles for the apartment that I needed. I opened the trunk of the car and put my weapon, my handcuffs, and my suit coat inside. My credentials remained in my shirt pocket. The FBI credentials were in a black leather case of such a size that about two inches of black was exposed above the pocket. Anybody who has ever dealt with an FBI agent would recognize a compatriot by that particular black leather clue. Well, there was a gentleman working inside the store who must have watched me remove my weapon and my coat and as walked in the store, obviously, saw the FBI credentials in my pocket. I passed the cashier and I was at the end of an aisle when I saw a man standing between the rows of goods. He had his hands up and he said, "You've got me. I'm not gonna resist arrest—you've got me."

I'm like what in God's name is going on?

The man said, "How did you know I'm working here?"

Well, I'm not going to reveal to the guy that I don't know what the hell is going on.

I said, "Assume the position. Put your hands behind your back," and I took my belt off and I tied his hands behind his back.

So now I've got somebody under arrest though I haven't told him he's under arrest.

"What's your name?" I asked.

He told me his name, but then he said, "But that's not my real name, that's just the name I'm using now."

"I want your real name."

Well, it turns out that this guy was not on the major flyer that we had, but he was wanted for questioning by several federal and local law enforcement agencies.

I walked outside with him, went to the car, got on the radio, called into the office, gave the code number for a background check on a suspect I had in custody, and told that I needed assistance.

A female voice came back: "In custody?"

"Yes," I answered.

"Is he under arrest?" she wanted to know.

"Yes," I answered. "Can you give me anything further?"

"He's using aliases—write these down."

I got my yellow pad out of the car and I wrote down the aliases she gave me, and I turned to the man in custody and asked him what name he was currently using and he told me. I went back on the radio and asked her if she had, say John Smith, on the list, and she said, "No," so I said, "Well, add that name to the list."

After a few minutes, I asked her to contact the unit coming to assist me and let me know their ETA and just who was coming. She said hold on and she was obviously calling the other car because I heard her call for a certain ME car and I didn't recognize the call.

Our ASAC at that time was a bulldog. I mean you made sure every "i" was dotted and every "T" was crossed when you wrote a report for him because he was a perfectionist. Nice gentleman, small, thin, and he wore glasses. If you saw this man, you would think he was an accountant or working in some insignificant job. You'd never put him down as an FBI agent.

It turns out that he was on his way to assist me.

Well, the estimated time of arrival was about five minutes and I just stood there thinking, Oh, my God it's him and no sooner did I have this thought than I look down the road and I saw this vehicle coming and sure enough there he was along with two other agents. These two agents immediately surrounded this guy, grabbed him, and one of them looked at the other and said, "Cuff him," and they put regular handcuffs on him. They gave me back my belt and the ASAC said, "I need you to be in my office in fifteen minutes." When I got back, I entered his office and he said, "I want to know how this all went down. I want to know every detail because I've got to make a report."

I received conflicting letters—one, congratulations for making the arrest, and two, a reprimand for being where I was not supposed to be.

Al Baldwin's next assignment was Tampa, Florida. There he rented an apartment and was immediately recruited to play on the complex's softball team. Later, in the midst of playing the game, he learned that Augie Busch, Jr. of the beer Busches played second base and, in fact, the complex was owned by Augie Busch. That became a problematic situation in that, as he came to discover to his discomfort, Busch was under investigation regarding a development on Paradise Island in the Bahamas.

After moving in, Baldwin checked in with the FBI office wearing shorts and a sports shirt. He had parked his vehicle on the street with his beloved Grady-White boat still in tow. He took the elevator up to the FBI office where he introduced himself to the receptionist as the new agent. He proceeded to give her his contact information.

She said, "Mr. Santanna has been waiting for you; let me tell him you're here."

Al protested: "No, no, I'm not dressed—I didn't come in expecting any formal meeting. I'm not dressed."

Ignoring his reluctance, she insisted that the new agent meet his new boss.

Baldwin knew enough about Santanna to know that he had been a professor of Spanish at the University at Bridgeport in Connecticut. Protocol dictated that Santanna would have Baldwin's file and Baldwin hoped their shared Connecticut connections might smooth his transfer. Alas, as it developed, Santanna had observed his car and boat from the window and his easing into the Tampa field office was anything but smooth. Certainly Santanna had his doubts about his new bachelor agent and the problems he might cause.

And Santanna did not want any problems.

He was on shaky ground with Mr. Hoover and wanted no further faltering on his career path to come to the director's notice. Santanna had lasted only a few months in his last assignment. That his aborted tenure was not his fault did not matter. The FBI had chosen to send him to San Antonio where General Santa Anna had once commanded the forces that took the Alamo, so his name was a source of local attention in that part of Texas.

Al related the circumstances of his initial meeting with the SAC:

He stood by the window and asked, "Is that your boat and vehicle parked there?"

I said, "Yes."

"Don't unhook it," he said.

I said, "Pardon?" to give me time to take in his order.

"Your stay here is not going to be long," he said. "When will you be reporting for work?"

"I can start tomorrow," I said, although my official start date was a few days away.

"Fine," he said.

The next morning, Al arrived and was assigned to work with another agent. His fellow agents were suspicious of him as agents were in those days suspicious of any incomer. You had to be sure he was not a spy for the Inspectors Unit. This unit was disliked by most field agents and had been dubbed "The Gestapo."

Before a newly assigned agent to a field office became part of that office's "family," he had to demonstrate over time that he was not a part of Felt's team sent out to spy and seek out any fault within a field office.

For example, each agent had two wastepaper baskets—one regular and one, painted red, was for confidential documents. Felt's plants would watch, and if an agent read a 302 and was spotted throwing it in the regular basket, the observer would be obliged to report him. If he didn't and it would ever get discovered, he would be in more trouble than the miscreant. He may not be fired, but he'd be disciplined.

The fear in those days was getting shipped to Alaska. Now that assignment is sought after. Every single hunter in the FBI wants Alaska.

In Tampa, it was not long before Al's association with the Busches came back to bite him.

Soon after I started in the Tampa office, the boss called me in and said, "Have a seat." And I sat down, and a guy came in with projection equipment and put up this film. It was a softball game, and as I was watching I suddenly recognized it was my condo team playing. "Oh, shit! There's me."

Santanna wasn't watching the film, he was watching me. He pointed and said, "You want to say anything?" And all I could say was, "I'm playing softball," and he said, 'We have an active file on him," and I said, "Who"? And he answered "Augie Busch, Jr.—he's a target in an investigation." There was a possibility that the Bahama project in which the senior Busch was involved was being financed by mob money and the question not answered was whether the son was also involved.

So then I had another mark against me as far as Santanna was concerned.

Al was in Tampa for several weeks when the SAC called him in to tell him that he was to be the new Special Agent in Sarasota, Florida. That single-agent office had responsibility for four Florida counties. There were agents sitting in that Tampa office who had been sitting there for nine, ten, twelve years hoping to get a shot at that residency. They asked themselves, "What's he got?" What they did not understand was that the head man was not promoting Baldwin—he wanted to get rid of him.

In no time, Al was ensconced in an office one floor above a bank in a corner building in Sarasota, Florida. He was all by himself with no one to answer questions and no files to peruse to learn how a veteran agent conducted an interview. But he was also in an office with no one to tell him what to do, no one looking over his shoulder, no agent in charge of an investigation saying, "I need you, Al, come on, Al, I need you to help with this arrest." He was his own boss; he could identify his own contacts; he could set his own hours. As a bachelor without commitments, he got more done from seven at night to three in the morning than he accomplished working from nine to five. And he got to work with the night guys who were making the arrests. He rode along in police cruisers and rode shotgun for highway patrolmen.

The only time he was not on his own was when there was a mass shooting or an officer down. Then every lawman in the area responded. Also, there were times when the Miami office might call for assistance. That happened if you had a fugitive on the run in the Everglades or hiding out with the locals. At that time, there were also a lot of Cubans in training camps in Southwestern Florida, and you didn't want to go into one of those paramilitary training bastions on your own.

The four counties under Baldwin's jurisdiction were Sarasota, Manatee, Desoto, and Hardee.

One of the first requirements for a field office in those days was to have three informants with a Russian background. There was no way in those four rural Southern counties that the Agent in Charge could do that, so Baldwin substituted informants with Klu Klux Klan ties. The South was loaded with covens at that time, even in Memphis there had been activity. There had been three civil rights workers killed in Mississippi while

Baldwin was in Memphis and he went down to help work that case. The bodies were found in earth mounds after Al had spent days in a swamp boat unsuccessfully dragging the swamp for corpses.

In the 1960s, Wauchula in Hardee County and Arcadia in Desoto still had posts where the local cowboys tethered their horses while they went into a café to eat lunch. A main road might be a dirt road and it appeared that on some days horses outnumbered the cars. Al remembers thinking, "My God, I've gone back in time to the 1800s."

Heeding another piece of advice from Julian Clark as to the importance of making friends with the local sheriff and how to go about doing so, Al always gave those county lawmen tokens of appreciation in the form of ammunition. They could always use additional ammunition.

Al discovered that a sheriff in a Florida county is one of the most powerful political individuals in the state and he set out to establish rapport with the four sheriffs in his jurisdiction.

A particular classification of cases designated by the number 42 was for deserters from any branch of military service. Proof that Al was successful in forging teamwork with the local sheriffs is in the outstanding record of success he established for 42s without ever physically locating one individual. Every time a sheriff's deputy apprehended a deserter, he would jail him on probable cause then call Al Baldwin to come and make the arrest. When Al arrived, he always did so with a case of shotgun shells or 38 ammunition for the office.

One time the head of the Tampa office called the agent in Sarasota and wanted to know how in God's name he could possibly go through so much ammo. He had an inventory sheet in front of him and fumed that no human being by himself could physically fire so many rounds in that period of time.

Al said, "I'm not firing it, I'm giving it away."

"You're what?" he growled.

"I'm giving it to the sheriffs and the police chiefs and certain deputies in the highway patrol, and they, in turn, help me on all my investigations."

There came a long phone silence before his superior gave up. "I'm not asking another question—it's approved."

Of course, he also had in front of him Baldwin's arrest record which reflected well on him. In the first six months, Al's numbers in some areas had exceeded the numbers the agent before him had achieved over his entire tenure.

Sarasota's bachelor FBI agent with the car and the boat that announced his eligibility was probably not without feminine companionship while a resident of that city. However, it was on vacation that he found the girl who took him to the altar. Al relates what happened:

I went home to Connecticut on vacation and, of course, immediately contacted my best friend, Bobby Mirto. Bob, like myself, was a bachelor, but he was on home ground and knew the singles scene while I knew no one to ask out. Since Bob wanted to go out on dates as a foursome, he, unknown to me, hatched a plan. One day when I was in his office, he asked me to deliver an envelope to the office of a friend. When I reached the address, I went inside to find, sitting behind the receptionist desk, this stunning blonde. As I was handing over the paperwork, I made a special point to examine her left hand and there was no ring. When I returned, Mirto asked, "Did you deliver the file?" and I said, "Yeah," and he asked, "Did anything happen?" and I said, "No, why?" and he asked, "Did you meet anybody?" and I said, "No," and he said, "You didn't meet the receptionist—wasn't she there?" and I said, "Yes, she was there." He said, "Her name is Georgeann Porto and she's single, Al, and she drives a Corvette." I said, "you gotta be kidding," and he said, "Do you want her phone number?" and I said, "Let me have it."

I went into another office and called her and told her who I was and asked if she'd like to go out to dinner that night, and she accepted and we went out to dinner that night and the next night we went out to dinner with Bob and his date, and every day for the next few days I went somewhere with her. When my time was almost up—although I had a two-week vacation, as was my habit I wanted to be back early—I said goodbye to her and asked, "Is it all right if I come up to see you again?" and she said, "Absolutely—and when I come to Miami I'd like to see you," and I said, "That will work, it isn't that far of a drive from Sarasota to Miami."

Well, I called her several times from Florida then. Maybe two months later, I get this call from her and she said, "How would you like to go out to dinner tonight?" and I said, "Where?" and she said, "Sarasota," and I said, "Who am I going out with?" and she said, "Me," and I said, "No way," and she said, "I'm here in Sarasota" and I said, "You gotta be kidding me," and it turned out she was checked into a local hotel.

The couple went out to dinner that night and the second day of her visit. Since she had a few more days to stay in Sarasota, Al convinced her to leave her hotel and stay in his condo. It was a new complex on the edge of the Everglades with a very nice swimming pool and was located across the road from the Bobby Jones Golf Course.

There was only one inconvenience: Al had noticed that a tent had appeared over the wires in the front of the complex, the kind of canvas shelter used by telephone repair personnel in inclement weather or to be somewhat cooler protected from the Florida sun. Al feared it was possible that this was part of a Mark Felt investigation of the local FBI office, that Felt's team was here in Sarasota to do an accounting of Al's office, Al's files, Al's personal ethics, and whether or not he was strictly following FBI procedures. So, during the first couple of days when Georgeann was visiting, the two used the rear parking area and the rear entrance. While she was there, the tent was removed, and Al breathed a sigh of relief.

By the time Ms. Porto returned to Connecticut following her Florida vacation, Al realized the relationship was serious. He took a short leave from the Bureau, journeyed to Connecticut and asked her to marry him. She accepted and they became engaged.

Even early in conducting the series of interviews with Alfred Baldwin that covered this period of his life, I found it odd that an FBI agent did not seem to know that his fiancé, Georgeann Porto, had mob connections. According to Al, he eventually learned that in Miami where she went after she left Sarasota, her uncles were quite prominent in the mob world. There were five brothers, one of which was her father. Though her father lived in Connecticut, his four brothers lived in Miami. Back in the late 20s, her grandfather had purchased a great deal of waterfront property on the lower East Coast of Florida. The sons now enjoyed the fruits of their father's investments.

Al decided to resign from the FBI, return to Connecticut, and marry. Over the next few weeks, he finalized that decision and returned to Connecticut to begin a new life as a married civilian.

4

AL JOINS THE COMMITTEE TO
RE-ELECT THE PRESIDENT

Naturally, Baldwin's recent stint with the FBI predicted success in looking into work in the security field. He began to interview as a candidate for several positions. One company of interest to him was owned by Clayton Gengras, a Republican who had made an unsuccessful run for governor of Connecticut. He had recently acquired the bus line that serviced the New Haven, Connecticut area, and he also owned the Adley Trucking Company in West Haven along with the Security Insurance Company.

Al interviewed for the position of Security Director for Gengras' trucking company and was hired and made part of his executive team. His first assignment was to ascertain the security situation at the newly acquired bus company and to ascertain that security at the Adley Trucking Company terminals was adequate. The latter task was of prime importance since that firm had a contract with the government to transport monies for the Federal Reserve. In an interview, Al was not sure of the full geographic extent of the service—if it were from Canada to Boston or if it went further south. Gengras wanted the movement of federal funds to be under tight security. Baldwin's initial task was to determine if an escort for the transfers was needed and, if so, if there was any way the company could get a government agency—either local or state police to assist.

Al was with Gengras for about two years and during that time had become a member of the Connecticut/New Haven chapter of the Society of Former Special Agents of the FBI. One of the benefits of membership was that the organization published a list of its members as a source of employment opportunities for FBI-trained security personnel. Pertinent information about a former agent's background and experience was on file and if your resume fit the criteria of someone seeking to hire, that resume would be referred to them.

A retired U.S. Navy Admiral was initiating a program at the University of New Haven designed to offer a two-year Associate degree to law enforcement officers. The Admiral planned to expand this to a four-year degree. He contacted Baldwin whose profile seemed to fit his needs and since the salary was considerably more than what Gengras was paying, Al accepted the employment offer to be his assistant for putting together the curriculum and for administration of this new college program. Al became one of the professors, teaching police officers in both Hartford and New Haven.

It was the late spring of 1972 and Al was enjoying the break between teaching semesters when the fateful telephone call came.

It was late in the evening, perhaps ten thirty, on Friday, April 28, 1972, when Baldwin's phone rang and he answered. He describes what ensued:

A voice said, "My name is James McCord. I got your name from the Society of Former Special Agents. I am Director of Security for the Committee to Re-elect President Nixon and I am calling to see if you might be interested in interviewing for employment with us."

We talked for several minutes. McCord asked questions and my answers must have been satisfactory as he asked if I would come down to Washington for an in-person interview.

My marriage during the late '60s had been short-lived and ended in divorce. At the time of the conversation with McCord, I was a thirty-year-old single man. I was ex-military, ex FBI. I had a law degree. I was in the fortunate position of having almost unlimited career options. One of the possibilities that I had been contemplating was to return to the FBI. However, given J. Edgar Hoover's strict rule limiting the time a resigning agent could reconsider a career with the Bureau to one year, and I had far exceeded that one-year rule, I had little hope of success. I discussed this with Mr. McCord and though he could not guarantee that I would be an agent again, he did assure me that if the president were reelected, people working for the Committee would enjoy precedence for obtaining government jobs and surely there would be a place for me in one of the security services.

This was a definite plus. I said the salary would have to be agreeable and he asked me what I expected, and he had no problem with the figure I gave him.

"Let me give it some thought," I said, assuming, naturally, that he meant for me to come down in the next couple of weeks. Hence, I was very surprised when he said, "I'd like for you to come tonight ... or tomorrow if that is possible."

"Let me call you back in a few minutes. I just need to make sure that my schedule is clear for the next few days." I knew it was, but I wanted to consult with a cousin of mine who was a prominent attorney in the New Haven, Connecticut, area who had Washington connections.

I reached him at home, gave him James McCord's name, and asked him to verify that he was who he said he was and to acquire any other pertinent information about the man. I knew my cousin had a friend who was a former agent working in the Washington, D.C., area.

He agreed and called me back after a few minutes and said, "Your Mr. McCord was an FBI agent, he retired from the CIA, he actually does exist." That confirmation and other information he provided gave me enough confidence to make the decision to go to Washington and do the interview.

I called McCord at the number he had given me. I was to learn later that it was his home number which I retained until a few years ago.

The last time I heard about James was in 2018. In his nineties, he was living with his daughter in a small Pennsylvania town on the state's eastern border. Sadly, I learned he suffered from severe dementia, perhaps Alzheimer's.

Baldwin disclosed that he called McCord back and agreed to go to D.C. When McCord said he wanted Baldwin to fly down that night, Baldwin countered that such a trip was impossible as there were no flights. He was taken aback when McCord said he would make arrangements and Baldwin should be at the New Haven airport at midnight.

Baldwin arrived at the deserted airport. Not a light shone in the closed facility. The entrance gate in the fence that surrounded the runways and buildings was padlocked. Baldwin waited, uneasy about the unusual arrangements. Time dragged as he paced but then a guard showed up to question his presence at the airport.

Baldwin explained but the guard was suspicious and gave him just a few more minutes before he had to leave.

About that time the two men both heard the unmistakable sound of an airplane approaching. Soon they spotted the lights of the incoming craft.

The guard unlocked the gate and in a few minutes the plane taxied to the unloading area, turned, the door opened, and the stairs appeared. The plane was a dark color and had no markings. A man in the doorway called "Mr. Baldwin?" Al answered in the affirmative and boarded.

He was met at Washington National and taken to the Willard. The restaurant was not yet open, but Al sat at one of the tables and waited in the low-light quiet. About the time the staff arrived and brewed the first pot of coffee, a man appeared. He was slightly balding, had very short-cropped hair. The suit he wore and the way he wore it told Baldwin immediately that the man was law enforcement. James McCord had arrived.

The two men talked for an hour or so and had breakfast. McCord directed Al to return to D.C. on the first possible regularly scheduled Allegheny flight prepared to go to work if his hiring was approved by a man he was to meet. Then Baldwin was driven back to National Airport and the anonymous plane ferried him back to New Haven.

Baldwin left New Haven on Allegheny's last evening flight to Washington, D.C., on Sunday, April 30, 1972. While airborne enroute to D.C., the aircraft developed a problem with a cargo door and the flight was directed to Philadelphia, Pennsylvania. After a short time at the gate and an announcement that the problem had been solved, the plane took off, only to be turned back again when the problem recurred.

Once the cargo door problem was truly repaired, the flight to Washington continued and the aircraft landed at Washington National after midnight.

Although McCord had advised Baldwin that someone would meet his plane, Al felt the long delay would have caused a change in that plan. Once he had deplaned, he set out to find a pay phone to call the number Mr. McCord had given him in case something went wrong. At this time, of course, there were no cell phones, but there were pay phones on every conceivable corner and in every conceivable place.

As Al was walking toward a bank of phones, he caught sight of an African-American gentleman dressed in a black chauffeur's suit with the appropriate hat. He held a sign on which was printed "Baldwin."

Al describes the interesting events of the next few days:

I approached the man and asked, "Are you here for Alfred Baldwin?" and he said, "Yes, sir, are you Mr. Baldwin?" and I said, "Yes," and, further verifying, he said, "You're to see Mr. McCord at the Committee to Re-elect the President?" and I said, "Yes, I am—that's why I'm here," and he said, "Follow me, sir—do you have baggage?" and I said, "No, sir, only what I'm carrying." He then proceeded to lead me out to a four-door black limousine.

He opened the back door for me, but I asked, "All right if I ride up front?" and he said, "Surely," and he opened the front passenger door for me and we drove through traffic across the 14th Street bridge toward Washington. McCord had told me that I had a room reservation at the Roger Smith Hotel and the driver acknowledged that he knew that was my destination.

I would later learn that the driver was a retired sergeant major or master sergeant from the Army, that he was Attorney General John Mitchell's driver, and that the limousine was Mitchell's personal vehicle.

I checked in to the Roger Smith, a hotel in downtown Washington. At the desk, I was given a message from Mr. McCord that he would meet me at the hotel the next morning, Monday, May 1, 1972, around 7:00 a.m.

I am an early riser and the next morning I was downstairs by 5:00 a.m. I went into the restaurant deserted even by the help. I sat down at a table that commanded a view of the front desk.

Maybe I sat there for an hour when I noticed a gentleman at the front desk. I watched as he spoke to the desk clerk and the clerk was picking up the phone when the man looked toward the restaurant. It was Jim McCord.

When he reached the table where I was sitting, he extended his hand and said, "Good morning, Alfred. Once greetings had been exchanged, he began: "Some questions."

I was to discover that James seldom spoke in full sentences. It was part of his persona to never waste time. He always spoke in abbreviated terms. I had also noted the very first time we met that he had an accent. I thought perhaps he was from one of the western states.

"Did you have breakfast?" he wanted to know. When I said, "No," he motioned to one of the help who had appeared, and they were coming and going as they prepared the room for serving. I ordered breakfast. McCord ordered coffee.

While I ate, McCord recited my date of birth, current address, current employment—all in short form as if he were reading from a form.

We were probably there for an hour before he said: "Time to go."

With that, he took care of the bill and we left.

"Let's walk," he said, and we proceeded up Pennsylvania Avenue in the direction of the White House. "I've made my decision," he said, "but there's another man who wants to meet you."

We were opposite the White House at Lafayette Square when McCord said: "Let's take a moment."

I followed him to a bench where we sat next to each other for a few minutes taking in the scene.

After a few minutes, he asked "Are you a religious man, Al?"

I thought about his question for a long moment, wondering from whence it came and what was behind it before I answered: "I believe I am. Yes, I believe I am." I might have said it twice.

There was another rather long silence before he half turned toward the statue of General Lafayette on his horse near where we were sitting. "A loyal and honorable man," he said.

"Lafayette?" I said, turning to look at the sculpture myself.

"Yes," he said.

After a few more seconds of silence in which I saw that he was staring directly at the White House, he said: "Not over there where you have disloyalty, no honor, and you don't have religious men."

I thought that was a strong statement for him to make to another, a stranger.

This exchange mystified me at the time. I came to look back upon it as being the first glimpse through a slowly opening door that would give me a sighting of James McCord's character. This exchange was the first of many which drew for me a picture of this man's patriotism and integrity. It was also an exchange that has stayed with me, as clear as a painting that once moved you. It is embedded in my memory to this day as one of the key clues to the why of Watergate.

I cannot say that I gave much weight to his comments at that time, taking them to be merely political. However, looking back on his words in later years, I realized the observations he spoke that day comprised the first piece in the Watergate puzzle. The Watergate epic, in my opinion, is like a puzzle and until all the pieces are in place, there is no clear picture.

He did not say another word after that statement until he said, "Time to go."

We continued to walk past the White House on the Lafayette Square side of the street, until we came to a multistoried building anchored by a bank on the first floor. The address was 1701 Pennsylvania Avenue. I would learn that the building was near enough to the White House that the iconic home of the president was part of the view from some of the Committee's offices. I would also learn that the floor above the Committee to Re-elect the President's (CRP's) space were the offices of a prominent law firm whose partners included the Chairman of the Finance Committee of the Democrat Party.

We entered, took the elevator to the second floor which opened into an entry. A man was standing in front of the glass doors that guarded a reception area. I could see letters on the glass. Either the man was painting "Committee to" on the glass or he was washing the glass. Anyway, he barred my view of the complete door.

McCord gave me a brief tour of the office layout. He pointed out offices along the main corridor, one of which he said was Jeb Magruder's who had come over from the White House to take the position of Deputy Director of CRP. He identified anyone we met by name and former employment. He would say "from the White House," or "He was with the president's security detail." Eventually, I learned that Mr. McCord had been with the Committee for about a year while the staff was being assembled.

Our tour ended at the office of the Director of Security. There were several desks, one of which was obviously prominent. I noticed several plaques on the wall in recognition of various services rendered by McCord to the CIA and the White House.

Stored in the office were various electronic devices, some quite large, maybe two to three feet by six feet by a foot deep. There were no weapons in sight but there were lockers that could have contained them.

I recognized Mr. Mitchell's driver seated at one of the desks.

McCord used the telephone on his desk before turning to me to say, "Come with me."

As we were walking down the hallway we had previously negotiated, McCord said: "I'm going to introduce you to the man who will have the final say as to your hiring. He is the attorney general's right-hand man."

I was dressed for just such an interview in the standard FBI uniform of dark suit, wingtip shoes, conservative striped tie, and, of course, a white shirt. Any FBI agent would have immediately identified me as a colleague.

We entered a fairly elaborate office with a name plate on the door that read "Fred LaRue." McCord introduced me to the man behind the desk who did not rise but did reach across to shake my hand.

I knew that Mr. LaRue was a trusted friend of John Mitchell and a confidant of the president's. I had heard he was from Mississippi and was very *wealthy. Meeting him now, sizing up his appearance, his demeanor, he turned out to be what I expected—a Southern gentleman.*

He did not ask many questions and what he did ask were fairly basic. He did ask if I were a registered Republican. My family had always been staunch GOP supporters so that was no problem.

It became evident that he knew something of my FBI career when he said, "Very unusual for someone in their second office assignment to become a Resident Agent." I explained about the unfortunately named Santanna and my theory that he simply did not want a possibly troublesome bachelor to bring Hoover's wrath down upon an already compromised Special Agent in charge of the Tampa, Florida, FBI office. He seemed to have some inkling of the nature of J. Edgar's rule and understood.

LaRue said, "I have one final question, Mr. Baldwin."

"Yes, sir," I said.

"Are you prepared to travel?"

"Yes, sir," I assured him.

McCord said, "His first assignment, if hired, will be with Mrs. Mitchell on her Midwest trip. Is there anything he should be aware of?"

Mr. LaRue asked, "Will he be armed?"

"He should be," said McCord.

LaRue reached down. I heard the sound of a drawer sliding open. His right hand came up holding a 38 snub-nosed revolver without a holster.

He did not proffer the weapon to McCord as an experienced law enforcement officer would. The cylinder was in place and I assumed the gun was fully loaded. Police officers are taught to always release the cylinder from the weapon so there is no possible way for an accidental discharge during the exchange. When the gun left LaRue's possession, it was in firing mode. Later that day, McCord passed the weapon on to me, again with no holster.

Mr. McCord thanked Mr. LaRue, took my arm and steered me out. He motioned toward the door meaning I should precede him. I did and he, closing the door behind me, remained in LaRue's office. I waited in the hall. In a few minutes he came out, shook my hand and said, "Welcome aboard."

I'm thinking now, "Oh, my God, I've just accepted this job."

It seemed very strange to me at the time and seems even stranger as I look back on it over the years that McCord seemed to have hired me without questioning me to any extent about my employment background or personal experience. I had expected him to ask about my duty stations with the Marine Corps and the length of time I spent assigned to different FBI offices. He had no questions about any of this. Neither did he seem to probe, as most interviewers do, for hints to my character. I believe he did not need to probe my experience as he had access to a CIA psychological profile. Expert psychologists at that agency were said to be able to predict if a man was going to be truthful and how he would act under various circumstances.

At a later time, James McCord would tell me, "I was impressed that you never used your famous great-uncle, Raymond Baldwin, to grease your career path."

We returned to the Security office where McCord introduced me to Robert Houston.

McCord left me with Houston while he tended to some business. Houston was quite knowledgeable. He went over the responsibilities of the Committee to Re-elect's security department and he filled me in on the idiosyncrasies of various CRP personnel. For example, I remember him telling me that one of the higher-ups preferred you not go beyond a greeting with him. He was leery of interacting with anybody he did not know well. He gave me these little insights about people with whom I would be working that would smooth my way. He also went into detail as to Mrs. John Mitchell's likes and dislikes.

He was candid about the deficiencies Mrs. Mitchell had found in the security men assigned to her for previous trips. It was apparent between the lines that Martha Mitchell had many fetishes. If her security agent stayed too long outside, she was angry. If her security agent wandered into the limelight, she was angry. One security person had failed to keep track of an attaché case that was important to her and the minute that trip was over, he was gone.

She insisted that her security remain within immediate eyesight as she would become paranoid if she turned to look for her security person and he was not in sight. You had to be careful if you were standing directly behind her as she might not be able to see you in that position. There would be major problems if she at any time lost sight of you. You must always stand where she can always see you. Her composure demanded that you be there for her anytime she needed you.

One of my primary responsibilities Houston failed to mention. Although it was an important part of my duties, he left it for Kris, Mrs. Mitchell's personal assistant, to tell me the secret of the infamous coffee cup. This cup, as I soon learned, never held coffee.

I was given some forms to fill out—a short application form for employment with the Committee to Re-elect the President—which became a major bone of contention when, after Watergate, CRP claimed I never worked for them. The application was definitely NOT for employment with McCord Associates, James McCord's private security firm. I also completed a standard form establishing the terms for withholding tax and social security deductions. I never was required to submit a substantive employment form or complete a comprehensive questionnaire that would have been routine in any normal human resources procedure.

I was also given papers that contained security procedures for the Committee along with an agenda for future plans which I was to review and comment on.

Later that day James sat with me and gave me some background information regarding his career prior to his employment with the Committee. He then outlined the basics regarding Mrs. Mitchell's Midwest and New York trip which was scheduled to depart D.C. on May 2. I would be assigned as her security agent on this fundraising trip.

At some point, I took advantage of an opening and asked McCord about the weapon he had given me. I raised the concern that I had no authority to carry that weapon without a license. I worriedly said, "I have no permit, nor do I have identification as a law enforcement officer authorized to carry a weapon."

I pointed to a display board on which a design of a Committee to Re-elect the President security card was posted. It was like a driver's license, marked to be produced about the same size, with a place for a photograph. I knew some personnel were carrying such IDs.

"Should I have one of those?" I wanted to know.

"Not at this time. Right now, we need you immediately with Mrs. Mitchell."

"But James—I'm going to have an issue with this weapon if I don't have some type of identification that substantiates the fact that I'm authorized to carry it. I am not an FBI agent. I'm not an active law enforcement officer of any type so I would think that a law enforcement officer or somebody stopping me would have a problem with me carrying that weapon."

He said, "It will not be an issue. There are two things to remember. One, you are working for the attorney general of the United States. The weapon is essential to your task of protecting his wife and other members of his family. No law enforcement officer in the nation should question that. Two," and he took a business card from his desk drawer and handed it to me. "Two," he continued, "if anyone questions you, give them this card and have them call the number on it."

In those days, flying was not as complicated nor were passengers herded like cattle as is the case today. You could simply walk into an airport and arrange for a flight—you didn't have to reserve and get there two hours early like you do today. You could get on a flight that was to leave in a half hour if you were lucky.

McCord's instructions about how to respond if the weapon Baldwin carried raised security hackles, were to be tested when Baldwin routinely flew Allegheny Airlines home to Connecticut and back to Washington.

There had been a few hijackings at that time, but as yet there was no equipment to check either passengers or baggage for means to take control of aircraft. Still, the incidents of planes being commandeered that had occurred had greatly alarmed the airlines and a new air marshal program had been initiated. Airline employees certainly evidenced an increased level of awareness.

For Baldwin flying in the spring of 1972, the drill went like this: When purchasing a ticket, he would advise the ticket agent he was carrying a weapon. When the agent asked for identification and authorization, Baldwin would answer that he was not currently in law enforcement, that he was a former FBI agent, and that he was part of the security detail with the CRP. With that, he would proffer the business card McCord had given him and suggest: "Either you or one of your supervisors should call this number for verification."

The agent selling tickets usually asked another individual at the counter to summon the appropriate supervisor. A few minutes later someone would join the agent at the ticket counter. The card would be passed on to this individual who then disappeared back through the door behind the counter to reappear shortly, return the card to Baldwin, and wish him a good flight. He would also instruct the ticket agent to advise the plane's captain of the circumstances.

Baldwin would board and almost always be directed to a seat directly behind the forward bulkhead. The door into the cockpit would be open and the captain usually had a few words to say like "We're glad to have you on this flight," or "I hope there will be no need for you on our flight." Perhaps airline personnel assumed him to be a marshal.

If he had to change planes, Al would be welcomed with "Mr. Baldwin, we're aware of your status," and would often be asked to board first. Sometimes the captain would meet him at the door and welcome him with a handshake.

Ending the first trip establishing this routine, Al Baldwin returned to D.C. on Monday evening, May 1. Again, he was met by Mitchell's driver and this time transported to the Roger Smith Hotel. He checked in and, since it was around 10:00 p.m., did not call anyone or go to the Committee offices.

5

AS MARTHA MITCHELL'S SECURITY

On Tuesday, May 2, Alfred Baldwin arrived at CRP offices and went directly to the security department. He began the day completing unfinished paperwork and preparing for the trip guarding the wife of the attorney general (AG) of the United States, a journey that would begin that day.

Mrs. Mitchell's agenda first took her to Grosse Point, Michigan, the suburb of Detroit where the auto elite maintained their mansions, via Chicago. There she was the honored guest and/or speaker at several events. From thence, the plan called for Mrs. Mitchell and her entourage to proceed to Westchester, New York, for additional appearances.

They were to travel by train which Baldwin found unusual. Posing a question to McCord about this out-of-date mode of travel, Baldwin was told, in that staccato way of his, "No flying. Flying is out. She will not fly."

Explaining further, McCord related the source of her fear of flying: Martha Mitchell had trained as a stewardess with Miami's Eastern Airlines.

In the course of training, she suffered, along with her group of trainees, a disastrous landing in a burning airplane. Although no one was seriously injured, Mrs. Mitchell had been so traumatized that she quit the program and developed a phobia about flying.[1]

In briefing Baldwin, McCord informed him that accompanying Mrs. Mitchell would be her aide, Kris Forsberg, of Greenwich, Connecticut. Forsberg was the daughter of the publisher of *Field and Stream* and *Outdoor Life*. She was married and had a young daughter of whom Mrs. Mitchell was especially fond. McCord also advised Mitchell's security man that local law enforcement at the various stops had been alerted, but, emphasized McCord, "You will be coordinating their assistance. You will be in charge."

Al interrupted his own telling of the tale on tape by remarking, "I remember thinking these lawmen were probably older and more capable than I. I'm thirty-six and too young to be in charge of old hands. Nor have I had any experience in this kind of assignment."

Baldwin asked James if there was a holster available for the snub nose and he said there was not. "Do the best you can with it," he said. The new security operative took that to mean to carry it in his waist band between belt and skin.

Baldwin had discovered that the snub nose was a very special weapon.

When cleaning it, he had spotted the serial number. It was a three to five zero number followed by the number thirty-eight, which was an extremely low number in a production line of weapons by Smith & Wesson. He speculated the gun had probably been given as a memento or a gift to someone of stature. Definitely, the 38 had a story. He had no way of knowing what that story was, but the gun was of some significance. Smith & Wesson would have taken care that a weapon with that low serial number

---

1 Mrs. Mitchell did fly in Air Force One as newspaper accounts reveal she was barred from this plane after making certain unscripted remarks to the press corps.

would have been presented to someone of importance they wanted to honor. How the revolver came to Fred LaRue, he could only wonder. But he did know he had better take very good care of it.

Al's conversation with his boss ended. Al continued his preparations for departure. Some change in the atmosphere caused him to break his concentration and look around. People were talking in hushed tones. There was an air of excitement. But wafting over all was a sense of confusion.

Something had happened.

He soon discovered what it was: J. Edgar Hoover, that legendary specter, that Sphinx of secrets that ran from the bedroom to the guarded center of government, the egotistic super patriot, the man deep in the closet— was dead.

The decision to be made was, with the demise of this singular American institution, should the arrangements for Martha Mitchell's campaign jaunt move forward or be cancelled?

In Alfred Baldwin's words:

Sometime later, McCord entered the office, approached Houston and me and announced, "It's a go."

He turned to me, took a stack of bills out of his pocket and counted out eight crisp new one-hundred-dollar bills which I noticed had sequential serial numbers. In 1972, eight hundred dollars was a sizeable sum, equal to several thousand of today's dollars.

He told me I should go to the Roger Smith, pack my bags, and return to the CRP offices.

"Need a ride?" he asked.

"Is time of the essence?" I asked.

"Yes," he said.

"Then a ride would help," I said.

McCord looked at Michell's chauffeur and said, "Take Mr. Baldwin to the Roger Smith and then to the Mitchell's."

After I gathered everything for the trip, Mitchell's driver and I followed McCord's instructions and eventually pulled into underground parking where the Mitchell's condominium at Watergate was located. I waited while the former Sergeant went upstairs and returned pushing a heavily loaded luggage cart. We transferred the assorted bags and cases into the black limousine. It was not long before Mrs. Mitchell and her aide showed up. I was introduced and then we proceeded to Pennsylvania Station in downtown D.C.

When I checked in at the ticket window, an AMTRAK official appeared. Mrs. Mitchell and Kris were treated to red-carpet courtesy. I went on ahead to inspect the quarters she was to occupy and the official escorted Mrs. Mitchell and her aide to our assigned track and car.

The arrangement of the car was a corridor with windows that flanked three staterooms. Each of these "cabins," if you will, had a seating area, a desk and chair, a lavatory, and a space where the porter would let down a full-size bed at night.

On our overnight trip from Washington to Chicago, Mrs. Mitchell occupied the center cabin with Kris' quarters on one side and mine on the other.

I posted myself in the corridor.

I was charged with the protection of Mrs. Mitchell's jewelry which I kept in a kind of belt wallet on my person the entire trip. In addition to inspecting any facility in which she was to travel before she entered, I was also to inspect any rooms she would occupy.

Kris was an accommodating person and graciously guided me in ensuring that Mrs. Mitchell felt secure.

One of the saddest aspects of Martha Mitchell's life in politics was her craving for recognition. (Oddly, at the same time, she reluctantly submitted to being photographed.)

On the trip I made with her, she expressed her disappointment in no uncertain terms. She felt she was being treated badly. Her unparalleled ability to raise the all-important early money that a campaign must have was key to the Nixon campaign. While I am sure she was acknowledged for her contribution by her husband and men like Fred LaRue, she received no thanks from the arrogant President's men in the White House. And I believe it was their praise and the president's recognition that she craved. There is a time in any endeavor when a little praise can stave off a lot of damage downpour. This was one of them. Just a few soothing words of gratitude could have avoided a whole lot of problems.

Although she had been very successful on previous trips and, exceeding all expectations, would raise some $400,000 on this trip, the White House seemed to take her efforts for granted and never singled her out for her accomplishments.

It was aboard the train that Kris revealed to me the coffee cup routine.

At the beginning of the trip, Kris gave me an attache' case which I must have with me at all times. In it were two bottles of Scotch. I must ensure that there were always two full bottles so that we never found ourselves in the situation where we were too distant from a liquor store for a refill. The two bottles were part of Mrs. Mitchell's way to cope. There was a special cream- colored coffee cup—another familiar totem—which I always carried. Whenever Mrs. Mitchell asked for a cup of coffee, I would pour straight Scotch into the cup, discreetly, of course, so that onlookers would not see the bottle. She might give me the signal from a head table, she might nod in my direction in a certain way when she was having a conversation—and I knew to bring her the infamous cup. It might be ten o'clock in the morning, two o'clock in the afternoon, 3:00 a.m. or 11:00 p.m., but if I got that nod or call, I got that coffee cup and filled it.

That evening, enroute to Chicago, the three of us went to the dining car about eight o'clock. Recognizing Mrs. Mitchell, a gentleman approached to ask her to autograph his dining car menu. When I moved to intervene, Mrs. Mitchell said, "No, it's all right." She was gracious, asked his name, wrote something, and he returned to his seat.

Once the dinner was over, Kris and Mrs. Mitchell went back to their car while I paid the bill. When I followed, their doors were closed but I knocked on Kris' door; she heard me from Mrs. Mitchell's suite, opened that door and said, "I'm here, Al."

"Is everything all right? Anything you need?"

"Could you ask the porter to bring some water?" she requested.

After making arrangements for that, I did not retire but monitored the corridor from the platform between cars for some time. I wanted to be sure that no one came along looking at the suite numbers or something like that. Just a simple standard security precaution. Sometime after midnight, feeling the area was safe for the night, I went to bed and to sleep.

I was showered, shaved, dressed, and at my post in the corridor when Kris, in bathrobe and slippers, emerged from her compartment around 7:00 a.m. to go into Mrs. Mitchell's room. She proved to be Mrs. Mitchell's alarm clock on this trip. I remained on watch until they both came out and we went to the dining car for breakfast.

Shortly after, we arrived in Chicago where we were to change trains for Grosse Point. No sooner had the train stopped than a Chicago police sergeant presented himself.

"Are you Mr. Baldwin?" he wanted to know.

"I am," I said.

"Anything you need?" he wanted to know, handing me his business card.

"I'm waiting for Mrs. Mitchell and her aide," I said, indicating their doors.

"Need assistance with the luggage?" he asked.

I answered in the affirmative because between them, the two women had a considerable number of bags—too many for one man to carry.

The sergeant summoned a porter who stood by on the near platform with a carrier. When Mrs. Mitchell came out, I knocked on Kris' door. The porter began to collect the baggage and I followed him through the rooms, making sure nothing was left behind. I then found my way to the accommodations on the Chicago-to-Detroit train, found no unwarranted devices, electronic or otherwise, no unusual packages, nothing that would indicate a threat.

I then joined the two ladies in an executive lounge where they had been taken by the Chicago police officer.

When the train was ready to depart, the officer led us to our car, the porter brought the luggage and I breathed a sigh of relief that everything had gone so smoothly.

Which proved to be premature.

The train had hardly begun to roll when Kris knocked on my door. I opened it.

"Do you have Mrs. Mitchell's hatbox with her wigs in it?"

"Her what?"

"Her hatbox."

"What is that?" I asked, my heart sinking.

Kris said, shaping it in the air with her hands, "It's a round case about like this—cardboard with a top on it. We can't find it."

"Where was it on the other train?" I asked. I could sense panic rising.

"In the closet," Kris said.

"What closet?" I wondered aloud.

I got into full panic mode.

There were two pieces of luggage in a storage space, so I said, "Give me a few minutes to check with the porter. Maybe it is with the large cases."

Although we were on an express train, the train did make one stop close to Chicago and we soon came to that stop.

While the train was at that station, I sprinted off the train, found a telephone, and dialed the number on the card the Chicago police officer had given me.

Luckily, I got him, and I poured out my story. I told him that Mrs. Mitchell's irreplaceable hatbox was on the train we had been on, the train that had now, if it had followed its schedule, left Chicago.

That worthy man said, "No problem. I'll handle it."

Subsequently, at our Grosse Point stop, the porter handed me the hatbox that was there on our arrival.

I later learned the sergeant had commandeered the Chicago Police Department's helicopter, and somehow had stopped our former train, after which someone went aboard her, went to our former car, and found the hatbox in the closet. Then the copter had flown to our destination, Grosse Point, and delivered that hatbox to ground personnel at the train station.

So, thankfully, Mrs. Mitchell's hatbox was no longer in a "lost" condition. As far as I know, she never learned it had departed our presence for a short period of time.

I have been told that wigs in the '70s were indispensable to busy traveling ladies. The complicated hairdos required rigorous maintenance and there was not always time between events for lady politicians or politicians' wives to properly rehab their coiffures. A wig ... and sometimes wigs plural ... were the answer to their recurring dilemmas.

After the hatbox was so miraculously bestowed, as if it were all in the course of ordinary events, I looked in on Kris and asked, "Do you still want Mrs. Mitchell's hatbox?" Kris took it with a wide smile and a "thank you." I *knew that somehow she knew something out of the ordinary had happened, but she never asked for details.*

As soon as I could, I called the sergeant and voiced my profuse gratitude. Among other things, he saved my job. I do not doubt that had I been held responsible for the loss of those wigs, I would have been fired. I would probably not even have been offered a ride from the Washington railroad station. When we returned to Washington, I saw that a letter to the sergeant's supervisor was sent, expressing appreciation for services to the Committee to Re-elect the President beyond the expected. In those days, very few thought to do that kind of thing, but I knew such a letter of commendation in his file could mean a great deal to the sergeant's career.

A grisly incident occurred on the leg of the trip from Chicago to Grosse Point. An individual was struck and killed by the train. We were inexplicably delayed for some time. I told Kris to tell Mrs. Mitchell there was a mechanical issue, but I also told Kris the truth and to make sure that Mrs. Mitchell remained inside her compartment as body parts were visible from one side of our car. After an hour while the incident was investigated, the train was permitted to proceed.

As to the people who played some part in Watergate, who later fabricated reports that I entertained Mrs. Mitchell with details of the tragedy, there is no truth to those reports.

When we arrived at Grosse Point, an FBI agent came aboard the car, and presented his credentials to me. He took Mrs. Mitchell and Kris under his wing and told me that they will wait for me and the luggage "outside." He was to drive us to the private residence where we were to stay while in Michigan. I checked all the compartments including the closets which were about the size of a large book and behind the lavatory doors—no wonder I missed Mrs. Mitchell's previous closet.

The porter and I left the train and found the limousine where the FBI agent was in the driver's seat and Mrs. Mitchell and Kris were in the back seat. The porter and I loaded the luggage, I got in the front passenger seat, and the agent accelerated and we exited the confines of the train loading zone. I noticed a city police car, manned by two officers, following us.

We were in a small business district when our vehicle was suddenly surrounded with bodies. There were hundreds of people with signs that read "Get Out Now!" and "Vietnam No!" and they were shoving themselves against the vehicle in which Mrs. Mitchell was riding and the police car, that was following us, was also stopped by the crowd. Our two-car convoy was surrounded.

We were completely engulfed by humanity, banging on the windows, shouting.

Mrs. Mitchell was showing signs of anxiety and fear; she was becoming highly agitated.

The agent said to me, "What do you want me to do?"

I said, "Go ahead very slowly. Let's not injure anyone. But do not stop again."

The agent edged the limousine forward and after what seemed like a long time, but was probably only a few seconds, we were free of the demonstration and moving at normal speed.

When I returned to Washington, I included the event in my report and I also recommended to McCord that the fact that the organizers knew of Mrs. Mitchell's arrival should be investigated. The fact that she was to be there was advertised by the sponsors of her speaking engagement, a Republican Women's Club, I believe, but her time and method of arrival had not been public knowledge. I believed that our security office in Washington should look into it and come up with some answers so that in future trips we could avoid this type of incident. I brought that out to McCord on my return. He felt the same as I did, that the details of our arrival had to have been provided by someone.

Mrs. Mitchell, Kris, and I arrived in the afternoon at the palatial residence where we were to spend the night. I believe it belonged to a member of the Ford family.

The first event was a private dinner in the home where we were staying. Mrs. Mitchell, family members, and guests of the family sat down to a very formal repast. Heeding Houston's instructions, I remained in the dining room standing to the rear and off to one side of Mrs. Mitchell, making sure I was always within immediate eyesight of my charge.

After dinner the entourage adjourned to a ballroom where a large group had gathered for a meet and greet with the honored guest, Martha Mitchell. A trio played background music to the polite murmur of conversation.

Unfortunately, I was plagued by one of the want-to-be-in-the-know types who, perhaps lubricated a bit too heavily at the open bar, was determined to find out what security agency I was with, what kind of gun I carried, had I ever shot anyone, had there been threats against Mrs. Mitchell, etc. No matter where I moved, this man pursued. I had little room to maneuver as I was limited to the space in which Mrs. Mitchell could see me. And at this particular function, she was constantly searching me out, making sure I was always within her beck and call.

The reception was over in an hour to an hour and a half. Everybody retired to their rooms. I had been given a room near Mrs. Mitchell and Kris and I stood outside until I felt she was secure for the night. No one bothered her. No one came to her door. After maybe an hour or so standing outside in the corridor I went to bed.

The next morning, I woke up early as usual. This was the day Mrs. Mitchell was to make her speech to the local Republican women's group.

Within the previous twenty-hour hours, the possible mining of the Haiphong channel was raised as a strategic option in the Vietnam war. This was the route that bore the most traffic in supplies from Hanoi. This was perceived by opponents of the war as an escalation of the conflict by Richard

Nixon. In response, a horde of reporters lay in wait for Mrs. Mitchell at the venue of the Republican Women's Club speech. This press attention was very unusual for this group largely ignored as they were unless a candidate needed envelopes addressed.

The Midwestern paparazzi felt the coincidence of Mrs. Mitchell's speech and the development in the unpopular war, happening around the same time, was an opportunity not to be missed. They were determined to corner her.

When we arrived at what had been viewed as a non-press event, the reporters were unrestrained. Mrs. Mitchell was petrified by the onslaught of shouted questions. Kris raised her arms in a protective gesture and said, "Hold on. Quiet down—she'll have something to say."

Mrs. Mitchell is looking to the right and left, obviously beset. Finally, she turned to me and said in an authoritative voice: "You handle this."

I shook my head. "I'm security. I don't talk to the press. I don't talk to anybody."

"You answer them," she ordered.

Well, obviously it was not my place to make any kind of statement to anyone. I was her security person and I wasn't in any type of advisory position. I was supposed to be invisible. I certainly was not supposed to make news. But I wanted to relieve Mrs. Mitchell. So, I said what I intended to be what any citizen loyal to the president might say. I have my quote written down because I had to repeat it in interviews with the FBI after Watergate and during the Congressional Hearings: "It is the president's decision based on advice after consulting with his advisors and his aides and thus there is no reason to question that decision at this point of time."

This seemed to assuage the reporters and I was able to get Mrs. Mitchell inside the building. Mrs. Mitchell seemed disturbed by the incident. She didn't like to have her photograph taken a lot and she didn't like being ... I use the word "hounded" by the press. She became increasingly nervous.

She asked for a cup of coffee. I provided it. She was able to deliver her speech which was well received. Conservative women of means liked Martha Mitchell.

Later that day, I received a phone call from Mr. LaRue, and he wanted to know the circumstances of my statement, especially why I had made it at all. I told him exactly what had happened, and he seemed satisfied with my explanation. I later learned that he was pleased with the way I had handled it. He wasn't upset. He felt it was a reasonable option given my dilemma.

We departed Grosse Point, proceeding to New York. We arrived without incident at Grand Central Station and were met by an FBI agent. After retrieving the luggage, we approached the vehicle indicated by the agent.

This was a most interesting vehicle. It looked like an official government executive vehicle that had once been of ordinary size but had been extended. I would learn that this was J. Edgar Hoover's personal car, that it was bullet proof and remained in New York City for his use when in the area. Hoover frequently came to the Big Apple during the racing season because he and his aide, Tolson, were both racing enthusiasts who frequently attended the horse track events in the New York area.

Since the Mitchells had lived in New York, where John Mitchell had been an attorney of note, the couple had many influential friends in the city and suburbs. Mrs. Mitchell was to be a guest at the home of one of her friends in Westchester.

I was sorry to see Kris depart for her Greenwich home while I remained at a local hotel in Terryville, New York.

In addition to the fundraising events scheduled for Mrs. Mitchell the next day, she was scheduled for a dedication at the Brookdale Hospital Medical Center in Brooklyn on the 8th of May.

As far as I knew those two days were without any special circumstances except for the alleged incident to be related below. The long week ended with a cocktail party hosted by close friends of Mrs. Mitchell in their Westchester home.

The next morning, Monday, I checked out of my hotel and returned to the residence where Mrs. Mitchell was staying. The FBI agent drove Mrs. Mitchell and me to Grand Central Station in New York City where we entrained for Washington, D.C. When we arrived in the capital, we were met by Mitchell's driver, Kris, and Kris' daughter. Mrs. Mitchell and the little girl departed in one vehicle while Kris, I, and the driver gathered up the luggage, loaded it into the limousine and then drove to the Watergate complex where Kris left the driver and me to unload while she took the elevator up to the apartment. She returned almost immediately to tell me that John Mitchell wanted to see me.

I was thinking, "Oh, my God—am I fired—what's going on—does he have a problem with something—what have I done?" as I accompanied Kris up the elevator that lead directly to the Mitchell floor. I entered the residence. I was met by Mr. Mitchell. He said, "I want to thank you—I've had nothing but positive reports on your performance." I said, "Thank you very much." He escorted me to the door, extended his hand and said, "Again, thank you," and I said, "Thank you, Mr. Mitchell," and I left.

When I got back to the Security office at the Committee to Re-elect after dropping off my bags at the Roger Smith, I was met by James McCord.

In view of the praise just received from John Mitchell, I was shocked when McCord told me, "Mrs. Mitchell claims that you removed your socks and shoes and put your feet up on a cocktail table in front of Secretary of Transportation John Volpe and she said that you are the most gauche person she has ever met."

I could only ponder the word "gauche." What could I possibly have done to earn that description? I was thinking, "What in God's name could I have done that led her to come up with that word?" I looked at all the possibilities of that word and decided there was no way.

I said, "First of all, I've never met, never been in the presence of, nor do I have any idea who Mr. Volpe is. I would take a lie detector to prove that, and if you want to administer a test, I'll take it because I have never been in the company of any such person."

"Good," said McCord. "I wanted to hear your side."

This was on a Monday and Mrs. Mitchell was scheduled to depart the following Thursday for a trip out West for another fundraiser.

I spent the day in the office composing memorandums as follow up to our trip. McCord had requested memorandums on several subjects: My comments to the press in Grosse Point, the incident of the pedestrian killed by the train, and a detailed report of the events at Grosse Point—all for the record. I also had to complete expense reports.

At some point, McCord told me, "You're not going to be traveling with Mrs. Mitchell on Thursday. Mr. LaRue is going to handle the schedule himself. However, I have other work for you. I need you to return to Connecticut to get additional casual clothes. You will be performing undercover work."

I was not taken off security for Mrs. Mitchell because of her "gauche" allegations. I doubt if anyone familiar with her emotional state at that time believed I was guilty as charged. To be charitable, her ranting was thought to be the result of her consuming too many cups of her unusual "coffee."

McCord himself never seriously questioned me about my relationship with her. After my denial of ever meeting Volpe, McCord nor anyone else ever referred to the fantasy episode again.

The truth is that everyone was concerned with Mrs. Mitchell's stability at that time. Her outbursts, her late-night telephone calls to reporters, her verbal rampages, her tirades, and her growing lack of control became increasingly damaging to the reelection campaign

From my balcony at the Howard Johnson, the balcony fronting the Mitchell apartment was in plain sight. I often saw a man in a suit on that *balcony and I would learn that a former FBI agent named Steven King had been hired to keep tabs on her. Years later, I read about the incident in California when she had to be physically restrained and King shouldered the blame for that incident.*

I believe she did know something that constituted a threat to the president. The president's men were very concerned about her lack of discretion. I don't know, of course, what secrets she was privy to but as the wife of the attorney general of the Unites States and a close personal friend of the man in the Oval office, she could easily have overheard critical information.

I know she knew some damaging secret closely guarded by Richard Nixon and his men. I know I was given specific instructions that if she strayed from her prepared text, if she crossed some invisible boundary drawn by her managers, I was to escort her from the field. I was to be especially diligent when she had imbibed several cups of "coffee."

When I returned to Washington on Friday, May 12, I returned to my new duties covering the anti-war demonstrations that were becoming increasingly worrisome to the government.

For example, Vietnam Veterans Against the War was on every security agent's radar. Rennie Davis' activities were of particular concern. There was talk of Jane Fonda returning to participate in protests. Ahead of me were two weeks of taking part in these demonstrations as an observer.

For the record, I want to state that I returned to Washington on Friday, May 12, 1972. The date is important because I no longer had a room at the Roger Smith. McCord had obtained a room for me at the Howard Johnson Motel on Virginia Avenue, directly across from the Watergate complex.

I was no longer within walking distance of the Committee to Re-elect the President offices.

The Watergate complex comprising offices, restaurants, a hotel, and private condominiums was beyond the Kennedy Center and toward Georgetown and Georgetown University. For those unfamiliar with the Washington area,

Georgetown is a town next to the District. It is characterized by upscale houses, upscale restaurants, and trendy shops.

6

UNDERCOVER AT ANTI-WAR DEMONSTRATIONS

A l Baldwin reported in at the offices of the CRP on Friday morning, May 9, 1972.

Having aroused the ire of Martha Mitchell, as had a string of bodyguards before him, Baldwin was persona non grata in the Mitchell camp. But perhaps because the CRP's security director needed his garrulous assistant to play the role of informer, a part assigned to him in McCord's surreptitious agenda, another job was found for Baldwin. McCord explained to Al what he expected of him in his new role: Dressed in casual clothes, he was to linger around the various groups that came to the capital to express the anti-war sentiment spreading and strengthening throughout the country. Demonstrations by some of these groups were planned for the coming days.

You have to go back to the turmoil that prevailed in that era to understand that the CRP had a legitimate interest in monitoring the activities of anti-war and anti-Nixon demonstration organizers in the general disquiet that plagued the nation.

The anti-war wave of demonstrations reached its highest level in 1972. There were threats to the White House and the campaign process that would culminate on Election Day, November 7, 1972. The security of supporters of the Vietnam War, the security of White House, and other government personnel opposed by the more militant activists was taken seriously. The many demonstrations taking place in downtown Washington that spring and summer were of concern to the government. The Washington City Police and the Park Police were using their resources to the hilt in maintaining order. James McCord, with responsibility for security for the CRP, shared an interest with the FBI and the Secret Service in the motives and plans of groups like the Minute Men and the Vietnam Veterans Against the War. Al was also to attempt to infiltrate any of those organizations that were considered potentially violent. He was expected to go to their headquarters and volunteer or in some way try to get inside information as to possible threats, bomb threats for instance, which might result in bodily harm or property damage.

A majority of the demonstrations would start at one location such as the Pentagon or the Washington Monument and end at another familiar site. Demonstrators would begin to congregate and when there was a sufficient crowd, they would form up and begin to move. Sometimes there were thousands of marchers. If anything from a confrontation to an act of violence occurred, the law enforcement agencies were ready to pounce.

It was rumored that on occasion, members of the security establishment would start a brouhaha themselves in order to have an excuse to break up a rally. A police officer who was part of the security at a major demonstration at the Pentagon told Al that some undercover officers had been instructed to initiate an incident so as to justify the police response that ensued on that occasion.

If the protest scene was quiet and the suspected radical organizations were inactive, Baldwin's instructions were to go to the Capitol Building and to relay information as to any anti-war activity in any of the Hearing Rooms or in the corridors of the House or Senate office buildings.

After making a round trip on Allegheny Airlines to Connecticut and back to Washington, D.C., Al arrived back in the Capital on May 12, 1972. He brought with him the necessary camouflage clothes suitable for blending in with the protestors.

Before actually joining the anti-war gatherings, he had lunch with Jim McCord at the Roger Smith Hotel. After lunch, the two men walked downstairs. James' car was parked in the garage and he paused before a barber shop also on that lower basement level.

Al related the ensuing conversation:

"Do you still have the weapon?" McCord queried.

"I do," said Al.

"Are you carrying?" he asked.

"I am," said Al.

"You won't be needing it so why don't you just give it to me now."

Al, following proper safety procedures, opened the chamber and removed the ammunition before handing the gun over. Years later, recalling the incident, Al expressed bewilderment that McCord chose a place in front of the glass window of a busy shop to request the exchange.

Later, at CRP headquarters, Al asked Robert Houston about the electronic equipment in the security department office. Houston explained that some of it was used for the daily sweeping of the CRP premises to make sure there were no wiretaps on the telephones, no bugs of any kind planted.

McCord had a rough sketch of some of the anti-war events scheduled for the coming days. Rennie Davis, one of the Chicago Seven and head of community organizing for Students for a Democratic Society, was to be in Washington and McCord wanted his appearance covered as well. There were other events in the list Al was to observe.

On Sunday, May 21st, there was a parade that started at the Washington Monument, proceeded down Pennsylvania Avenue, and culminated on the steps of the Capitol. There protesters were regaled by Bella Abzug, a New York liberal of the day, who accused Nixon of acting illegally in his recent decision to mine North Vietnam ports. Also speaking were Rennie Davis and Dick Gregory, the former a veteran of the anti-war demonstrations at the 1968 Democrat convention in Chicago, the latter a popular black comedian who had turned to political activism. The following Sunday, protesters including Dr. Benjamin Spock again gathered at the Washington Monument, paraded up Pennsylvania Avenue to the Capitol. On Monday, May 22, anti-war organizers planned to keep Pentagon employees from going to work by forming a human blockade of the giant building.

Al talked about his experiences during this period of reconnoitering the protest scene following daily instructions directly from James McCord:

On assignment, I wore a fatigue jacket, old military trousers, and some boots I had retained after leaving the Marine Corps. I had used these clothes for working so they looked worn and I fit in with the protesters very well.

Once, I joined the buildup for a large demonstration on the grounds of the Washington Monument. When enough people had gathered, we formed a parade which was to make its way down Pennsylvania Avenue to the White House. I actually marched arm in arm with a Jesuit priest who had taught a class I attended at Fairfield University. I remember, as we passed the Department of Justice, looking up to see Attorney General John Mitchell standing on one of the building's balconies along with some aides and I remember wondering what the AG (attorney general) was thinking. It was strange not to see Mr. Hoover out on his balcony. There were a great many photographers on the other balconies taking pictures of the demonstrators as we walked by.

One night after a march some protesters stayed overnight on the grounds of the Washington Monument. A few found shelter in small tents they had obviously brought for that purpose. The National Park Police did not seem to object to the makeshift sleeping arrangements, and I saw no one removed.

I believe the attempt to block Pentagon workers from making it to their jobs went on for some two hours. There were people making speeches throughout the crowd, but no one was paying much attention.

Apparently out of nowhere, but really out of the woods surrounding the Pentagon, galloped a dozen or so horses carrying Park Police and other agency law enforcement personnel. Mounted police descending upon a crowd is a powerful incentive to disperse. And disperse that crowd did.

I was among those running away and along with others was grabbed by police officers posted along a predetermined perimeter. Once in custody, you were taken to a holding area before you were herded on to one of many buses assembled for transportation of those arrested to a jail. In that time frame, the government was using every such facility available in the Washington area whether it be military, federal, local, or state—all were overflowing.

I carried a business card blank with a phone number printed on it, and I had been instructed to use it if I ever ran into such a situation. I had used it before so when I ran to the perimeter where officers were waiting, I gave the card to one of the officers escorting me toward a bus.

"Could you make a phone call? Can you call this number and tell them I'm a government employee," and that's actually what I said, "government employee—covering the demonstration."

I was led aside and left for a few minutes standing in front of a school bus with another officer. As I waited, I observed several people being led to the school bus while the main body of people were forced to board one of the regular city buses.

Soon the officer who had taken my card returned, nodded to the officer who was holding me, and said, "He gets on the school bus,"—and I did.

I took a seat across from three men. I kept glancing at them on the trip from the Pentagon into Washington. They looked familiar. I identified them as the same three men I had observed at the Washington Monument. Of course I could not look into the future, but it would include this trio of Metro Washington police officers arresting the Watergate burglars on the morning of June 17.

The bus stopped in a secure area of D.C. and the driver said, "O.K., everybody out." I remember it was a parking lot. All of us got off and began to scatter in different directions.

On those days that I worked a demonstration undercover, around 5:00 p.m., or at a convenient time toward the evening hours, I was instructed to call in to the CRP on a direct line to the security department, to make a report as to what was going on that particular day. If you arrived at nine thirty, for instance, you made a report around noon, another between three o'clock and four o'clock, and, if the event continued, still another between seven o'clock and eight o'clock. Of course, I had to seek out a public telephone as did other undercover agents who were also infiltrating the protests. We all sought out phones near the Washington Monument and at generally the same time. It was natural that I began to identify other law enforcement types calling in situation reports on the day's events just as I was doing.

One night, I believe it was a Tuesday, probably the 16th of May, James sent me to the headquarters of the Vietnam Veterans Against the War. He gave me their address and told me to volunteer. He wanted me to learn if any part of their program included intentions of causing property damage. I did as he instructed, and I did discover they were aware of the Committee to Re-elect offices on Pennsylvania Avenue and planned a demonstration there. I tried to get a specific date, but they were being tight-lipped about that detail although they were discussing the target quite openly.

It was over the next several days of meeting with and working under the instructions of James McCord that I really began to learn what the man was all about. In addition to our close working relationship, I was invited to the McCord's suburban home in the evening hours on two, maybe three, occasions. Observing James in his home environment amidst his family gave me even more insight into the character of the man.

I believe the first time I went to McCord's for dinner was one night during the week beginning Monday, May 8, after my trip with Martha Mitchell.

James drove me to his home. It was a two-story, brick Colonial on a cul-de-sac at the end of a street in Rockville, Maryland. There was a patio on the back of the house accessed through the kitchen and through a den.

James's wife, Sarah, was most cordial. She led the conversation over dinner. She asked questions about my background, my family, my schooling. I felt she sincerely wanted to know about my life and my interests.

After the dinner was over and the table was being cleared, James said, "Let's step outside."

The brick patio was circular and welcoming. We sat in comfortable chairs and I could see that the backyard was bordered by a wooded area. There were no streetlights to mar the stars of a beautiful spring night.

After James made a few remarks about the next day's schedule, there was a silence while we both enjoyed the view before he spoke again.

"I know yours is a political family, Al, and I know you taught school. Did you study political science or history?"

I may have said, "Some or a little." I don't remember.

"Have you ever thought about how a president is removed from office?" he asked next.

I guess I looked as if I didn't know where this conversation was going, which was the case, so he clarified: "How can a sitting president be removed?"

"He dies," I said.

"No—that's not removal," James said.

"Well, there's Amendment 25," I said. *Amendment 25 governs what happens if a president is disabled.*

"No, that's not what I'm looking for," James said.

"A military coup," I offered even as he shook his head at that idea.

"No," he said, "That isn't possible in the United States. If it were Europe, yes, a military coup could work. Our military is not strong enough.

"Assassination," I said.

"No, Kennedy's assassination left too many questions unanswered. And it happened too recently. Not good to have another assassination so soon."

"You remove him by voting him out," I said, "but that has to be done on a specific date."

I'm thinking, what is this about—what is he driving at? "He could resign, I guess," I said.

"That's true, but no president has ever resigned."

"You've got me—I have no idea," I said.

"Impeachment," he said. "How about impeachment—if he is impeached or threatened with impeachment and he feels he doesn't want the facts to come out in the process, he would resign before being impeached."

Another piece to the "puzzle" is put in place.

Al could offer no reasonable explanation as to why McCord brought up the subject of removing a president from office. He was totally unprepared for his boss interjecting various scenarios of aborting a president's term. There was no connection between the conversation and his suddenly introducing this line of questioning, and he offered no reasons for it after the matter was dropped. "You know," he said, "it's not really money that controls power—it's information. I learned that very early in my career, Al, especially during World War II that the individuals in government who control information have the power and of course power gives you money."

He paused, then continued with: "Hoover knew, and Nixon knows the power of information and both men knew how to use it."

There was a long pause while I was thinking, "What the devil is he getting at?" Then he continued: "In the security field, in intelligence gathering it's all about information. When I came back from World War II, I was with the Bureau for a number of years and then I went over to the CIA."

And I said, "I'd read that, James. I read somewhere in your background you had been for a number of years with the FBI both prior to and after World War II and then you left and went to the CIA. What actually gave you the initiative to make that move?"

James brought up the name of Wild Bill Donovan who was the head of the Office of Strategic Services (OSS) during World War II. I had always been interested in military history and, especially, Medal of Honor recipients. Knowing that "Wild Bill" had received a Medal of Honor, I asked James, "Did you ever meet Bill Donovan?"

He replied, "Now there's a person one would be honored to work with," but he never answered whether or not he had actually met or worked directly with the founder of the OSS. But then he went on to say, "I had the chance to meet and work with several OSS types and some Russian intelligence people."

He paused and I said, "I didn't know you had an OSS background."

"No, I was in the Army Air Force, but I met Dulles and Helms from the OSS."

There was a long pause as we sat looking at the edge of darkness that was the woods.

"Knowing and working with those men helped me to make my decision as to what I would do after the war's end."

McCord was neither a braggart nor arrogant. When he spoke, he was always direct and to the point. Over the period of our working together, I *learned he never repeated himself, and he communicated so that repeating himself was never necessary.*

Martha Mitchel

Al Baldwin's first assignment with the Committee to Re-elect the President was to act as security for Martha Mitchell, the wife of then Attorney General John Mitchell. In 1972, Mrs. Mitchell was making appearances across the country raising money for President Nixon's campaign for a second term in the White House.

Photo National Archives/Wikimedia Commons

Alfred Baldwin testifying before the Senate Watergate Committee May 25, 1973. Robert Mirto, his friend and attorney is on his right.

An AP Photo.

James McCord meets reporters 1973. On his left is Gerald Alch, his attorney; on his right is Sam Donaldson.

Washington Post Photograph by Harry Naltchayan

Al Baldwin telling his story in 2018

7

THE JAMES MCCORD I KNEW

F rom personal observation, I began to form an opinion as to the character and personality of the man who was James McCord.

I knew he was born and raised in Waurika, Oklahoma, a small town
on the Oklahoma–Texas border. South of Waurika is Fort Worth, Texas, one
of the most interesting towns in the Old West and a center for the history of
the American cowboy. Also, Waurika was located on the old "Chisholm Trail,"
that famous route used to drive herds of cattle north from Texas to Kansas.

There is no doubt in my mind that James was much affected by the
reality and the myth of the cowboy character. He was born in 1924, several
decades too late to be one of the storied cowboys himself. But he was definitely
a product of "cattle country." I know for a fact that when I look at an archived
video of him walking down Pennsylvania Avenue toward the Committee to
Re-elect the President office, I can see beneath the city clothes the cowhand
in a long-sleeved shirt and spurred boots moving down an unpaved street in
Oklahoma armed with the certainty of integrity. In high drama moments,
his mouth curves slightly upward toward his right cheek, a signal that he was

bemused by the people around him doing exactly what he expected them to do.

If you grabbed a still photograph off that clip—that is James McCord.

In that same video of him following a news camera focused on his figure, he has a trademark expression that says, "If you only knew what I know." His mouth is set in a turn that is not quite a smile—it is just an upturn on one side—but it says, "I wish you knew what I know."

Under pressure, he always had a very confident, knowing set to the lips.

Like John Wayne or Kevin Costner playing a cowboy role—purposeful, honorable, straightforward.

McCord was a taciturn man; he did not talk in sentences like a Washington suit but communicated in sometimes curt phrases.

Aside from the lopsided lip expression, McCord had another "tell." To give himself the seconds he sometimes needed to regain control of a situation he would reach into his pocket, take out a piece of hard candy, put it in his mouth, and savor it for a short time. I saw him demonstrate this "tell" several times.

The first time was when the staff of the Committee to Re-elect the President were in the throes of uncertainty after the unexpected death of J. Edgar Hoover threatened upheaval to the schedule. I saw Jim sitting at his desk and he put a piece of hard candy in his mouth, and he just sat back, and his mouth was moving, and he was like a different Jim McCord ... it was like it calmed him down and Houston, obviously excited, came in with his hands waving and complaining, "Jim, we have no idea what's going on!" and James, very steady, held up his hand palm outward and said, "Don't worry about it. Don't worry about it." His manner said he was in control and everything would be all right.

Another time he took to the hard candy to bridge a bad moment was when he called me "Al" instead of my alias when first introducing me to Liddy and Hunt.

Still another occasion was when I watched the BBC broadcast of 1993 chronicling Watergate. I saw him take a hard candy during an exchange with John Dean. I knew he had no use for Dean.

Jim McCord was a man one trusted. He was likeable in a distant sort of way. You wouldn't get in his space. He was the only man in her husband's D.C. circle of whom Martha Mitchell was fond.

He was a patriot. He was proud of the CIA and protective of its unfettered mission.

I did not know James McCord before he recruited me to work for the Committee to Re-elect the President nor was our personal connection of long duration, but there developed an unusual closeness. This man with so many experiences—think of the war years, the FBI, the CIA—would come to share a great many stories with me. In hindsight, it is quite possible that the revelations were deliberate shards, planted for me to piece together in the light of later events.

He was definitely a unique individual. I began to recognize that during visits to his home. There, he was his silent cowboy self, leaving it up to Sarah, his wife, to carry on a conversation.

But after dinner, we'd go out on the patio and he would talk to me as if he had known me for twenty years. It is amazing to me how he treated me. He brought me into his confidence. He divulged a side of himself he did not show others and I felt it was all leading somewhere, but I did not know where.

I look back now, and I am totally convinced he had a very specific agenda and I had a part to play in his plan. There were several occasions that he could have easily terminated my employment. After the Martha Mitchell trip when I came up short in her estimation, he could have said, "I'm sorry, Al, that it didn't work out," and I would have been gone. But he didn't. No *matter what occurred, he stepped right up with another slot for me. It was like he never allowed anything to interfere with my continuing to work with him.*

Throughout the period, when I was undercover at anti-war demonstrations, I had daily contact with him. Over the time of monitoring Democratic Headquarters, we spent long hours together in the motel room at Howard Johnson's.

All the literature on Watergate identifies Liddy as the decision-maker in the espionage assault on the Democrats. Liddy himself says he hired McCord because he could not find anyone else who possessed the electronic expertise for bugging. In my experience, it was James McCord who was in charge.

The night of the planned entry into McGovern headquarters, it was McCord who said, "We may have to abort." It was not Liddy.

My respect for James McCord continued to grow even after his arrest through our extensive telephone exchanges.

Internet sources record that James McCord joined the FBI after college and took part in searching for German spies in the United States before serving in the U.S. Army Air Force (1943–1945). In 1948, he returned to the FBI but went over to the CIA in 1951. In 1962, he became senior security officer in Europe which also led to his working closely with MI5 in England. Later, he was responsible for security at CIA headquarters at Langley. He retired from the CIA in 1970, founded his own security firm, and then was recruited for the job of security director for the Committee to Re-elect President Nixon in 1972.

McCord's coming out of retirement to sign on with CRP has a problematic odor. He had a long and distinguished career in the intelligence field culminating in retirement from a high position in an organization with global reach. To agree to oversee security in a political campaign seems an illogical career move. He was financially secure, and with his Wild West heritage a sensible last chapter would have begun with him riding into the sunset. On the other hand, perhaps the CRP opportunity was a reasonable step given his mission. That he had motive to accomplish that mission will be disclosed by Alfred Baldwin as an integral piece of the puzzle that was Watergate.

McCord always insisted that the CIA had no involvement in Watergate. As the White House conspirators moved to use the CIA in the cover-up, McCord wrote his letter that warned "if Helms goes, and if the WG (Watergate) operation is laid at the CIA's feet, where it does not belong, every tree in the forest will fall. It will be a scorched desert. The whole matter is at the precipice right now. Just pass the message that if they want it to blow, they are on exactly the right course." In February of 1973, Richard Helms was replaced at the CIA. The following month, McCord wrote a letter to Judge John J. Sirica which opened the way for prosecution of All the President's Men.

The cadre of men who mounted the covert entries into the Democratic Headquarters were not a cohesive group even though almost all had CIA backgrounds. E. Howard Hunt disparaged McCord's expertise and professionalism and thought McCord's job as security at Langley had been a mere routine job of checking offices after hours. Hunt described him as thick-necked, wide-jawed, and a casting directors ideal of a thug. G. Gordon Liddy denigrated his "wire" man, McCord, as a bungler who was always doing things to sabotage operations: bringing transmitters that were not charged, failing to remove the tape on the doors, always appearing and disappearing, ever overcautious. The two shared the same cell after their convictions and Liddy suspected that the ordeal of arrest, defending himself, then preparing for appeal had caused McCord to lose his mind.

Of course, we have observed that McCord was contemptuous of the Liddy–Hunt twosome and kept his distance from them and Hunt's Cubans.

Outside sources who support Baldwin's belief that the removal of the president was a goal of a junta in the CIA include Carl Oglesby, the author of *The Yankee and Cowboy War*, who argues that McCord was part of a CIA plot against Richard Nixon. Oglesby has gained support for this theory from former CIA officer, Miles Copeland, who claimed that McCord had led the Watergate burglars into a trap. The journalist Andrew St. George suggested that CIA Director Richard Helms had prior knowledge of the Watergate break-in.

Al Baldwin, in telling of his part in the mythopoeic that was Watergate, consistently makes a distinction between a CIA operation and an operation using CIA assets. Some observers point to the CIA tactics of misdirection, alternative paths of evidence leading to different conclusions in the aftermath, trails of bread crumbs left through labyrinths—all part of the tradecraft of "intelligence." With all the probes into Watergate, all its mysteries have yet to be solved.

James McCord died on June 15, 2017, almost to the day of the 45th anniversary of the famous burglary where nothing was taken.

8

THE MOVE TO THE HOWARD JOHNSON

On or about Friday, May 12, 1972, on instructions from McCord, Al Baldwin moved from the Roger Smith Hotel to the Howard Johnson Motel (HoJo) on Virginia Avenue, a few blocks from Georgetown and directly opposite what was called "The Watergate Complex." He occupied Room 419 which overlooked Virginia Avenue.

When the adventure of working for the CRP began, not all of Baldwin's interests were political or operational. He had noticed a woman who also worked in the 1701 Pennsylvania Avenue building which housed the CRP offices. They sometimes shared an elevator, his destination being the second floor, hers the third. She was very attractive, and she appealed to him. One day when they happened to be on the elevator together, he did not get off at his floor but stayed in the elevator. She got off on the third floor and he saw that opposite to the opening elevator doors was a suite of law offices. He rode the elevator to the top floor, but on the way down, he stopped at the third floor where she had exited.

Al relates what happened:

I wasn't dressed, I was still in the casual clothing of my undercover disguise when I entered the law office on the pretext of locating a fictitious character. When I entered, I saw her standing at the receptionist's desk. Sitting at the desk was another lady.

I asked my bogus question and got an answer from her before I asked, "Could I speak with you a second?" and we moved away from the reception desk and I said, "We've crossed paths several times and I'd just like to know if maybe someday you might like to have lunch or something," and she said, "That's a possibility," and I asked her for her name and phone number. She went back to the reception desk and I saw her take a piece of paper and she wrote down something and then she came back and handed it to me. When I glanced at the paper, I saw written on it her name and phone number. I looked at her and said, "I'll call you."

I did call her the next evening, and we made arrangements to meet at a restaurant she recommended that was close to her apartment. I had to call for a taxi to get to the restaurant where we were to meet. We enjoyed a pleasant evening and after that anytime my duties permitted, we'd go out. As I did not have transportation, at some point she offered to drive in and pick me up and we had more choices of places to go. I had not used my real name with her but as we became closer, I did tell her that I had not done so because of the nature of my work. I did tell her that one day I would let her know exactly who I was and what I was doing. She let me know that from the very first time she saw me, she knew I had something to do with law enforcement or security and that I was probably working for the Committee to Re-elect the President.

Sometimes I would go up to her office and we would go to lunch. On one of these occasions, she introduced me to her boss who turned out to be Robert S. Strauss, a leader in Democrat politics. At the time I met him, he was the Treasurer of the Democratic National Committee and later he became that organization's chairman. Strauss was also a former FBI agent.

President Richard Nixon was to leave the country on or about May 21, 1972, for a summit with Russian leaders in Moscow. He was going to be flying from Andrews Air Force Base. McCord had information that there would definitely be a demonstration at that base on Saturday, May 20, and he wanted me to cover it. Reluctant to depend on the inconvenience of cabs, I called my friend on a Thursday night and asked if she were going to be busy on Saturday and she said, "Why?" and I said, "Is there any chance you could pick me up in the morning, we'll take a ride out to Andrews Air Force Base, go to lunch someplace, and spend a day together?" And she agreed to do just that.

She picked me up on Saturday morning around 7:30 a.m. She was driving her Volkswagen. It was raining hard—one of those drenching down-pours that make you think there's going to be another flood. We arrived at a gate at Andrews Air Force Base which I know is not the main gate. I saw no signs of a demonstration. I talked to a guard at this gate who immediately asked for my identification. I gave him my Marine Corps ID and he saluted and said, "How can I help you?"

I said, "I'm looking for the main gate. There is supposed to be a demon-stration out here."

He gave us directions and we soon arrived at the main gate which was wide open. A guard waved us through, and we drove to where Air Force One was parked on a runway. The rain continued unabated and there were men taking refuge under the fuselage of the big plane.

I asked my friend to park outside a gate that was open to that area of the runway. I looked around and there was no one in sight except for the personnel under the plane preparing the craft for flight. I looked around again and noted that there was not one demonstrator in sight. They were supposed to be there by the busloads. I didn't see any buses waiting to disgorge the hordes.

I left my date and chauffeur in the car, saying I wouldn't be long, and started walking toward the aircraft to see how close I could get before somebody saw me and stopped me.

I was about halfway to the aircraft when out of nowhere came this vehicle with red lights flashing. It turned out to be Air Force security personnel, not the Secret Service and they came down on me like cat on a bird and the next thing I know they had me in custody. They took me to a security area in a building where I was joined by my friend who had been taken from her Volkswagen and into custody as well. A plainclothes individual who turned out to be a Secret Service agent wanted to know just what in God's name I was doing there at the airfield in close proximity to the president's plane.

I started to explain to them I worked for the Committee to Re-elect the President and I was there to be sure there was no demonstration or security risk and if there was any demonstration or security risk, I was to report it to the head of security for the Committee. I reached in my pocket, took out the business card and said, "If you would call this number, I think it will establish who I am and why I'm here."

I turned to hand the card to a full Air Force Colonel who was present and had been leading the questioning.

The Colonel took the card. I believe this Colonel was in charge of the security at Andrews, and he was at the office that weekend due to the fact that the president was scheduled to arrive and depart for his trip. In a matter of a few moments, the Colonel came back, talked to the Secret Service Agent, and then handed me the card and instructed his men that these two individuals can go and suggested strongly that we leave the base immediately. I said, "No problem."

They returned all my personal effects they had taken from me; they returned her personal effects including her pocketbook and wallet. I was certain that the questioning had probably revealed my identity. As she drove back to Washington, I filled in some of my personal history. We made plans to see each other again but Watergate occurred, robbing me of any further opportunity to see her.

Her name came up during the FBI's investigation of me and my activities in Washington, so obviously she was contacted by the Bureau. I know for a fact they were satisfied with whatever information she gave them. From the time she dropped me off after our Andrews adventure to today we have never spoken nor seen each other. I find myself wondering whatever happened to her, what her life turned into after she had the encounter with myself. In case it would embarrass her, I do not want to reveal her name.

Things were quiet on the demonstration front after the Pentagon Blockade of Monday, the 22nd of May, and President Nixon's departure for meetings at the Kremlin. For the next couple of days, I spent quite a bit of time at the Committee to Re-elect Headquarters, and I made some uneventful trips to the Capitol building.

On Tuesday, the 23rd, I had dinner with the McCord's. James asked me about my car, and I reminded him that it was still in Connecticut. At that, he said, "I want you to return to Connecticut and bring your vehicle back." That is exactly what he said—"I want you to return to Connecticut and bring your vehicle back." It never dawned on me to ask him why. Yet, there was really no apparent reason for having my car in D.C. However, I knew he had a reason. That was the way James handled himself. So, on that Wednesday, I flew Allegheny home once again to pick up my car. In the early hours of June 17, 1972, as I fled D.C. in that automobile, I would come to know why he knew I would need transportation.

And another piece to the "puzzle" would fall into place.

Since Baldwin left his car at home rather than in long-term parking, he called his friend Bob Mirto to pick him up at the New Haven airport. The two friends caught up with what had been happening in their respective lives before they parted. Al did laundry and repacked his luggage before driving his car to Washington on Friday, May 26.

9

EAVESDROPPING FROM HOWARD JOHNSON'S

I n 1972, a drive from New Haven, Connecticut, to Washington, D.C., took about six hours. I arrived back in Washington on Friday, May 26, 1972, around 1:00 p.m. I used my key card to open the door at HoJo, Room 419. My very ordinary motel room had been transformed into an extraordinary electronic laboratory.

On the side of the typical motel room where a bureau with drawers is connected to a bench that runs the length of the wall, there was side by side equipment. Some of it I remembered had been in the security department at the CRP offices.

James McCord was in the room, fiddling with a dial on one of the units of hardware.

James said, "Get yourself set up and I'll explain what's going on here."

Having driven for hours, I needed to freshen up, so I took a shower and got dressed.

James began to briefly tell me the function of some of the apparatus. There seemed to be two units which were receiving devices, one larger than the other, some six feet long, four to five feet high, and a foot to a foot and a half deep. It had a reel-to-reel assembly.

On the front of another unit, there were dials below a window with an arrow in it. This unit was grey and had what I took to be a USN inventory number on a piece of paper stapled to its side. It had a cover you could close, and it would look like an odd-shaped suitcase.

James's hand was on one of the dials and as he turned it this way and that, a needle in the window moved up and down.

As he fiddled, I heard various transmissions: exchanges from aircraft landing at Washington National, destination addresses for cab drivers, all kinds of messages emitting from this device.

He said that he was looking for a specific frequency and I watched as he searched patiently for more than an hour. James took off his headphones so I could hear the transmission.

I remember when he found it. A humming sound came on crystal clear.

James said, "Got it."

It was on 118.9 megacycles. I have never forgotten that number. It was the frequency of the Gemstone Files. It was the frequency that broadcast the conversations I subsequently monitored and whose content I typed. This was the frequency that captured the transmissions from the Democratic National Committee whose offices took up the entire sixth floor of the Watergate office building across the street.

The exchanges logged in by me became the Gemstone File. Gemstone would become synonymous with espionage.

The name "Gemstone" came from the plan drawn up by Gordon Liddy in response to a need for legitimate campaign intelligence operation. That Liddy's original plan, presented to John Mitchell, John Dean, and

Jeb Magruder on January 27, 1972, was way beyond legitimate opposition research is part of accepted Watergate history. Each plank in the program was named for a gem: ruby, infiltration; emerald, a spy plane; quartz, telephone tapping; sapphire, use of prostitutes; crystal, electronic surveillance; garnet, counterdemonstrations; turquoise, sabotaging air conditioners at the Democrat's convention hall; topaz, photographing Democrat documents; opal, break-ins. The plan was rejected.

On February 4, a revised, scaled-down plan was presented and also rejected. However, on March 30 at Key Biscayne, a third whittled-down plan was presented and apparently approved.

James McCord told Al Baldwin that he attended a meeting chaired by AG John Mitchell while he was still the AG, in which the plan was discussed. McCord told Baldwin about some of the discussion of targets for surveillance, phone taps, and break-ins. McCord also told Baldwin that John Mitchell had made it clear that the president wanted intelligence as to the Democrat's strategy in the upcoming election as well as the campaign plans of his opponent.

These revelations by McCord to Baldwin of the details of future political espionage approved by the highest law official in the land had two important results: One, it gave Baldwin the assurance that listening to the conversations on the tapped phone was legal. Two, in the aftermath, it gave Baldwin the wedge to gain a promise not to prosecute by asserting he could put Mitchell solidly in the arc of Watergate.

Baldwin stubbornly refused to disclose to this interviewer what was said on the tapes, claiming he was still subject to a federal court order sealing that material. He does contend that there is nothing on those tapes that would have made any difference in the outcome of Watergate. The nature of the information on those tapes provided limited enlightenment to the President's Men who were trying to determine what approach to take in the upcoming campaign between Nixon and his Democrat opponent, who would be McGovern, in the race for the presidency.

In fact, as the information on the tapes was passed on, Liddy judged the operation to be useless. McCord, however, felt the information gained justified further monitoring.

Al related what happened that day the bug became live:

That afternoon, it was maybe 2:30 p.m., and we could look over and see people working in the offices of the Democratic Headquarters. James had his attention locked on the dial when all of a sudden, the speaker in Room 419 sounded a ring and then a female voice said, "Oliver's office," and both James and I looked over and saw a woman standing in front of the window. There was a door out to the balcony and this door was open. She walked into the doorway and looked directly over in our direction. She had the phone to her ear and from what I could hear on the receiving unit, I realized we're listening in to her conversation. There was this woman across the street and somehow we're hearing this conversation between her and somebody else. She is explaining that a certain individual won't be back in the office until Monday so could she take a message and have him call.

James adjusted the volume so we could hear, but I think you would have a tough time hearing if you were on the other side of the door trying to listen.

Whoever the caller was said, "No, I'll call Monday," and I watched the woman put the phone down and the machine was silent.

James just sat back in his chair, folded his arms, and a little smile came on his face and he looked at me and said, "It's working."

I said, "What's working?"

And he said, "We're going to be monitoring the conversations on that phone."

And I'm thinking—at this time, 1972, it was not illegal to wiretap a phone if you have the consent of one party so obviously McCord has consent. Nor was it illegal if done in the interests of national security, or on the authorization of the attorney general. No way it could be illegal I told myself. James had told me that Attorney General John Mitchell had recently chaired a staff meeting at the Committee offices, while still the acting attorney general, and that a plan to install wire tapping devices in the Democratic National Headquarters (DNC) was discussed and approved by him. According to James, this subject was then discussed in other meetings with the attorney general. Also, you have to remember there was a mentality back then that seemed to justify the means used to obtain information. McCord used to say, "There's always a war going on." We were the good guys. No one questioned it.

James said that the telephone being monitored was in the offices of the Democratic National Committee. I got no explanation from him as to our purpose in listening.

But whose office was it?

It took a little while to establish that.

A voice would say, "I'm on Spencer's phone." Another voice, another time, would say "I'm using Oliver's phone." Some callers would ask for "Spencer," others for "Oliver," or even just "R." Initially, we thought the secretary might be working for three different men.

We did not have the Internet, research engines, reverse telephone capability in 1972. But McCord obtained a paper directory of the Democrat Party officials and found an R. Spencer Oliver, a deputy director in charge of the Democrat State Committee Chairmen across the country. As the contact person for the various state organizations, Oliver was in a position to aid McGovern whom he apparently favored. His secretary, we determined, who was also assigned to that phone, was Ida Maxine Wells.

To this day I'm still confused as to whether it was really Spencer Oliver's phone or Ida Maxine Wells' phone. An odd thing was that the telephone was not on a desk but kept in a desk drawer. When people used this phone, they had to open a desk drawer, take the phone out of the drawer, and then place it on top of the desk that I have to assume was Ida Wells' desk and then it went back into the drawer when the conversation was over. I remember that constantly happening. Every now and then the phone would stay exposed on the desk.

The Democrat convention to choose a challenger to Nixon was coming up in July 1972, in Miami, Florida. Any information as to who this would be was important to Republican strategy. Besides McGovern, several other candidates were in the running for the nomination.

It is important to note that we had successfully established an electronic connection with Democratic Headquarters, though not via Larry O'Brien's telephone, prior to Friday the 26th of May. The media and history have the first break-in and the first plant of a listening device on Sunday, May 28. This cannot be correct since there had been an entry prior to May 26th, and McCord and I began listening that Friday, May 26.

After verifying the successful connection, James, in his cowboy style of communicating without complete sentences, told me that two men would be coming to the room. Because of the nature of the work we were doing, he wanted me to use an alias and I chose "Bill Johnson." (Bill Johnson is a cousin of mine who was a lieutenant in the West Haven Fire Department.)[2] He also told me our visitors would be using aliases as well. Around 6:00 p.m., the two men came to our motel room, and James said, "Al, I'd like you to meet," and he stumbled then, realizing instantly he had blundered in using my real name. I don't remember exactly how he recovered but he got through the introductions and then explained briefly the purposes of the various instruments.

---

2 When Al Baldwin's use of his cousin's name came out in the coverage of the Watergate trials, his cousin, Bill Johnson, called Al's mother and said, "Tell Al I'm not mad at him for using my name." Rather, it seemed to have given him a certain notoriety he enjoyed.

As the two men, who I would later know as Gordon Liddy and E. Howard Hunt, were leaving, James said, "I'll be there around midnight and we'll make contact."

Everybody shook hands and as the two men left the room, he turned to me and said: "We're going to be working late tonight—are you all right with that?" and I said, "Absolutely."

Observing the three men together as James demonstrated the functions of the equipment, my feeling was that James McCord was in charge. Body language and attitude gave me the sense James McCord was the head honcho.

From Room 419, I could not only view the office where the phone we were monitoring was located but the reception area was also visible, and I could see people come and go. That first Friday night of observation and monitoring, James and I watched as a lady came down the corridor, turned off the lights, and locked the front doors. Although we had "line of sight" over to the DNC offices, I could tell that McCord, for some reason, was not completely satisfied.

James said, "That's it—we won't get anything else."

We went to dinner. Having dinner with James McCord was like having dinner by yourself. No idle conversation.

Back in the room, he proceeded to give me a lesson in Electronic Devices 101, instructing in more detail the functions of the various equipment. He also removed a few devices stored along the wall that had not yet been opened and explained to me what they were designed to do.

"You've got two units across the street, one of them is definitely not working and I've got to do something about that," he said. "Maybe it is shielded." And at the time I didn't understand what the term "shielded" meant, but eventually James explained to me that if you put a listening device say between two steel beams, those steel beams can act as a barrier and not allow transmission from that device to the receiving unit unless you are underneath it or very, very close by.

It struck me then that somebody had to have gone into Democratic Headquarters and installed those two devices he was referring to.

By that time, it was about 11:30 p.m. and James said that we were going out, that he had to pick up some items in an electronics store and then we were to meet some people. He did not say who they were.

"We'll take my car," he said.

I stayed in the vehicle while he got what he needed at the store.

It was just before midnight when he came back and drove toward the Capitol.

"Do you know anything about McGovern?" he asked.

"Yeah," I said, "He is one of the Democrat hopefuls for the upcoming election."

"We have a man working in his office and that's where we're going."

About this time, we were just about adjacent to the Capitol building. The area surrounding the North face of the Capitol, looking away from downtown Washington, was, at that time in 1972, not a particularly safe neighborhood. Yet the homes looked solid with two levels offering two housing units. The buildings were Victorian, very close together, without front lawns to speak of. The McGovern campaign had leased one of these houses.

As we drove by, James said, "That's it."

There were lights on the upper floor, and he added, "Our man is still working."

I'm trying to figure out what is going on.

James said, "I've got to go up a different street—they're not where they are supposed to be."

Which makes me even more mystified.

We go up a street and James brakes and stops alongside another car. James' car has a front bench seat. A man gets out of the other car, opens the front passenger door of James' car, tells me to slide over, and he gets in.

So I'm now between McCord and another man I will eventually learn is G. Gordon Liddy. He was one of the two men who had visited us earlier that evening at our motel room.

We drove back to McGovern headquarters, the light was still on but there was a man, probably a drunk, sitting on the concrete in front of a store that is about three doors down. We circled the block. The lights were still on at McGovern Headquarters, but the derelict had not moved from his post and James voiced the opinion that we may have to abort.

There was a row of bright lights going up a driveway adjacent to the building that housed McGovern Headquarters.

"I'm going to have to take those lights out," Liddy said. He opened his briefcase and I looked down and saw a pistol, some type of high-powered air gun. He took the weapon out, but James said, "No, no, that's not going to be a good move," and Liddy obediently put the weapon back in and closed the case.

(Unbeknownst to McCord and Baldwin, Liddy and Sturgis would return to successfully shoot those lights out as related by Liddy in his book *Will.*

McCord said, "Let's take another drive by."

We drove around the block returning to find the derelict was still there but the lights in McGovern Headquarters were now out.

"Where's our man?" asked Liddy.

McCord said, "Don't know," and then after a moment, "It's a no go—we can't risk it. That's it for now."

We took Liddy back to his car, he got out, and said tersely, "I'll be in touch."

Once he had closed the car door, I looked at James and he sighed in relief. "Idiot," he muttered. "Amateur," he added then he said, "Let's call it a night."

James was driving down the street next to the Capitol building. It was on a hill, and at the base of the incline, there was a traffic light and it was red. He just drove right through it. Immediately, there was a squad car behind us flashing its lights.

After James stopped, the officer came up, looked in the window and asked, "License and registration." It's two-thirty in the morning and here are two well-dressed sober men. You can tell he knows this is no ordinary stop.

James handed over his wallet and said, "My fault, officer—I was talking to my friend, and I wasn't paying attention."

I don't know for a fact whether or not there was anything in the wallet that identified James as Security Director, Committee to Re-elect the President. I assumed there was just a regular driver's license from the state of Maryland.

Yet, the officer handed back James's wallet, James said, "Thank you," and the officer said, "Drive safe," and walked away. There had to be some type of message that this officer viewed that caused him to let us off.

I said, you didn't use the Bureau or CIA ID and he said, "No," just "no," and we proceeded back to the Howard Johnson's where he let me out and said, "Get some rest and I'll see you tomorrow—" No, he said, "I'll see you later today."

The next morning James knocking on my door woke me, and, after a shower and a shave, I took over monitoring the conversations. This routine would be repeated in the coming days.

The setup across the way in the Democratic Headquarters puzzled me. Different people came into the room to make calls on the telephone containing the listening device.

I said to James, "They've got to have their own phone in their own office—why the hell are all these people using this phone? Here it is Saturday and there shouldn't have been anybody working over there and yet there must have been a dozen people using this one phone and I'm like "What's the attraction of this phone?"

James just smiled and said, "Don't look a gift horse in the mouth—take what you can get."

The same was true in the early evening hours. You might see a light go on way down the hallway and all of a sudden somebody would pop into this office and use this one particular phone. Now and again, a caller would hang up and put the instrument into the desk drawer and you could actually observe the next person walk in, open the desk drawer, take the phone out, put it on top of the desk, and dial their number and we're listening to the dialing on the receiving device. A problem developed with the reel-to-reel recorder, so James asked me to take notes. "Take down as much of the conversation as you can," he said, "I am terminating the recorder."

After writing down the gist of several exchanges, he reviewed what I had recorded and said, "This is good." And he left me to it.

As I have said, to James's disappointment, a second bug that had been planted in what was thought to be Larry O'Brien's office was inoperative. Another entry had to be made to establish a connection.

Instilled in my mind even today is the fact that there had been an entry prior to May 26 and after and yet, in the various histories and memoirs of Watergate, those entries are ignored.

I know for a fact that James McCord, and probably others, had made an entry to the Democratic National Committee offices at the Watergate Complex prior to May 26. This entry had to have happened without incident because McCord never discussed it and there he was on Friday, May 26th, listening to a device over at the DNC. How, when, and who made this entry will probably never be explained.

There was also another entry between May 26 and June 17, 1972. I actually observed McCord inside the DNC office area. McCord appeared inside Ida Well's office. At one point, he stood clearly visible to me in an open area and looked directly over to where I was standing. I believed then, as I do now, that this was a deliberately planned act on his part. If it was anything else, it would not have been a good move for a "super spy."

Toward the end of May, it became obvious to McCord that we needed a better line of sight and he arranged to move to the 7th floor. This was the top floor of the Howard Johnson with only the rooftop swimming pool above it.

We moved all the equipment to Room 723. Some of it remained encased; in fact, some of the cases were never opened, and the individual devices that were in use were placed for operation on the desk-like furniture in the new room. From Room 723 you could see the balcony of the Mitchell's condo and you had a clear view of the street side offices at the Democrat office. However, an office that was not visible was Chairman Lawrence O'Brien's.

I was responsible for the continuous monitoring of the conversations on the telephone in Spencer Oliver's office. As long as there was anyone in Democratic Headquarters, I was listening. McCord might spell me, but the surveillance was constant.

My mornings started early. I ate breakfast before business hours, and I was at the receiving station when the first employee arrived in the Democratic Headquarters across the street. I never left Room 723 until everyone had departed and the offices were completely dark and deserted. Our location afforded a clear visual of the main reception area and we could see the woman whose job it apparently was to lock up every night. Or, if someone stayed late, we could see that person turn off the lights, lock up, and exit the suite.

Even when the Headquarters appeared closed and I went to the Howard Johnson Restaurant to eat, I occupied one of the booths along its front windows. From this vantage point, I could see across the way and would know *if lights came on signaling that someone had returned to the Democratic National Committee offices.*

There were days when the telephone that held the listening device was so continuously busy that Baldwin and McCord subsisted on the snacks and sodas that were available in the coin machines in the motel's hallways.

This writer speculates that the telephone was a dedicated long-distance line, perhaps a Wide Area Telephone Service (W.A.T.S.) line, a service in those days that allowed for great savings on long distance calls. McCord also believed that calls on that telephone did not go through the office switchboard, providing privacy to callers.

Most of the time the employees at Democratic Headquarters left around 5:00 p.m. There would be a few stragglers that were apparently more dedicated. Then, too, we can assume that many of them continued exchanging views in the Democrat Tavern, a private club for the Party's politicos situated in the basement below the Party offices. In the Tavern, employees of the National Party could be joined by elected officials and staff from the Congressional offices on Capitol Hill.

Over those first two weeks in June, James McCord spent a great deal of time with Baldwin in Room 723. Early on, McCord began to tell his assistant some of his experiences in the security field. He talked about how much he learned in World War II when, in the later days of the conflict, he was involved in Army Air Force intelligence and had met his counterparts in the OSS. Its founder, Bill Donovan, had pulled together experts from all walks of life, from academia to zoology, to mount espionage operations to help win the war.

McCord made a point of referring to his early acquaintance with Allen Dulles and Richard Helms, both then young men like himself, working in intelligence. From what he told Al, it appeared that he, Dulles, Helms, and other individuals involved in the intelligence field had worked together in Europe during and immediately after the war's end.

Al remembered:

McCord told me that the bonds he had formed with these men amid the drama of war were of a special nature. Even some of the Russians in the KGB were among those with whom he had formed a special relationship fueled by the intensity of the times. This kind of attachment, James felt, was something more than any that might be formed in civilian life.

By the 1960s and 1970s, a cadre of those Americans who had been the foot soldiers doing intelligence work during the occupation had moved into the higher echelons of national security organizations. This was also true of some of the Russians. James led me to believe that some of the camaraderie between the patriots of the two countries endured across the years of the Cold War. Contact was renewed periodically when certain Russians came to that country's embassy in the United States.

One day, McCord would talk about the European situation after the surrender and when Germany was divided amongst the four allies. The next day, he would take up where he left off so over the two weeks, a continuous narrative was delivered.

The subject of the Russians was a major thread that ran through McCord's disclosures over the two weeks in which we spent so much time together in that motel room. At first, I thought that his monologue was simply a man recalling stories to fill the time between listening to the conversations on the telephone across the street. As time went on, however, I began to see a pattern in his divulging so much about the Russians that I had not known and that what he was telling me was profoundly connected to what we were doing.

On one occasion, McCord referred to my surveillance the day Nixon was to travel to Russia. He prefaced his remarks with words to the effect that with government nothing happens overnight. Nixon's trip, he said, had been in the "planning stages" for years with the goal of adding the immense Russian market to the consumers of American corporate goods and services.

No doubt the CIA had knowledge of these possible trade agreements between the United States and Russia pursued by the personal diplomacy practiced by the Nixon–Kissinger team. I gathered from what McCord said that at the very least the CIA monitored the situation.

But, he cautioned wearily, "Nothing is free, Al. Everything has a price." That statement was followed by a considerable period of heavy silence. I kept hearing what he said and the way he said it over and over in my mind for several days. After all these years, I can still hear it.

A little later, McCord referred again to trade negotiations. Now plans included opening Red China. He ended this disclosure with a heartfelt "My God." Then silence.

I began to feel that he was deliberately telling me about events and experiences that he wanted me to remember. It was as if he was opening a history book for me to hear. He never came out and said he had a purpose, but that he had one, I did not doubt.

Much of what he said had "integrity" at its center. That word kept coming up. He might refer to a person who had "integrity," and then follow that with a remark about someone who exhibited no "integrity" in his dealings.

James McCord, continuing the conversation that took place over a two-week period, related that he had come home from Europe to rejoin the FBI. He had been an agent when he volunteered for active service. Later, he left the FBI in 1951 to join Allen Dulles at the Central Intelligence Agency (CIA), the successor agency to the OSS.

Allen Dulles was deputy director of the CIA from 1951 to 1953 at which time he became director. James McCord placed Dulles in the category of the good guys—among men of integrity. Dulles, in turn, was quoted as ranking McCord, "the best man we have." Helms had nothing but praise for McCord when he became director at CIA, a position he held from 1966 to 1973. He had been an OSS agent in Europe during World War II and after the war had joined the newly formed CIA.

James McCord ended up as Director of Internal Security at Langley, the home of the CIA. He had to be more than just an electronic expert to be in that position. During his tenure, there was no record of a defector going over to the dark side.

At some point in this long, drawn out record of James McCord's experiences related to Al over their hours together, Al began to believe that what he was saying was not just words to fill up the time. He had an agenda.

Aside from the theme of integrity, a second thread that ran through McCord's narrative was the influence of big business on foreign policy. He voiced his concern about Nixon's rogue diplomacy, how in personal meetings with the Russians, he had made concessions in order to convince the Soviets to allow American companies to operate in their country and to market goods to their citizens.

Al relates:

Jim McCord told me that the price of Nixon's success was high in terms of human life. Nixon had revealed to Russian authorities the names of Russian government officials having friendly ties to the United States security network. Some of these men who were McCord's friends from the war years simply disappeared. I believe he said fifty-three had disappeared but I cannot be sure of that number.

Another piece of the puzzle slides into place.

We were steadily listening and logging the conversations which I would later divide into three categories: personal, political, and sexual. But James continued to express disappointment that the other device that had been placed in Democratic Headquarters, the one that was intended to monitor Democratic National Chairman Larry O'Brien, was not transmitting. McCord said regretfully that another entry would have to be made to correct that situation.

I think it was that same night that he talked to me about Liddy and Hunt's break-in at the office of Daniel Ellsberg's psychiatrist. He was most derisive of their escapades, recalling that they had their photographs taken in front of the building, wearing disguises, and making such a comedic mess of the whole operation.

About eight-thirty one evening of that first week in June, McCord and I were wrapping up. The last person had left the offices across the street. It seemed to me we were going through an ordinary end-of-day routine when James said, "I've got something to do. I'm going across the street. I'll be back in a few minutes." He started out the door, turned to me and said, "Keep a sharp eye out."

He left. I stepped out on the balcony.

After a few minutes, I watched him cross Virginia Avenue. There was no mistaking him. His manner of walking, his crew cut over bald head, his suit. I followed him visually until he disappeared into the lower garage of the Watergate building.

Probably a half hour went by. Then a light went on in Spencer Oliver's office, the office in which we had for days observed people talking on the telephone while we took notes on the content of their calls. We could look straight into this office. There was also a doorway that led to a balcony outside that office.

I was looking at this office when the lights came on behind the blinds that covered the windows. As I watched, the blinds went up and there was James McCord standing in the window. I had an absolute clear view of him. I was staring across the street at him and I know he was looking at me.

Suddenly, the blinds went down, but the lights stayed on.

Some fifteen minutes went by before the blinds went up again. I saw a figure, back turned toward me, which could only have been Jim McCord. Seconds later, that office was dark, but I could see James standing at the door that led to the balcony.

There were still lights on somewhere in the interior. McCord turned away from the door and disappeared. All the lights went dark.

It was perhaps a half hour later when McCord returned to Room 723.

He never referred to his foray across the street. He said not one word about entering Democratic Headquarters. He never asked if I had seen him. He never said anything about what he did over there. The only thing he said was, "Now we will see if the unit is working."

I asked, "How will you know?"

He answered: "I'm going to have to scan," and from the cases we were not using, he retrieved a piece of equipment similar to the one we were using to listen, and he took the cover off the machine and he began to set it up— plugged the cord into the power outlet, took out a set of earphones and began turning the dial trying to establish contact for what I believe was another unit he had obviously gone over there to place. He was not successful. He stayed with it for at least an hour or two. I would say around midnight he called it quits, and said, "I'll see you in the morning," and he left.

After he was gone, I thought about the fact that someone had to have gone into Democratic Headquarters prior to the 26th of May or I would not have been able to hear the Ida Maxine Wells answer the phone used by her and take messages for Spencer Oliver that afternoon when I returned from Connecticut. Since I was not a witness to that entry, I could not provide any information to anyone about it. Now, I was a witness to James McCord's entry that first week in June of 1972. What possible explanation could there be for the elaborate operation to follow on June 16/17?

But that was in the future.

The day after McCord slipped in and out of the sixth floor of the Watergate office building, (it might have been the Wednesday or Thursday of that first week in June) he came to Room 723 and spent several hours trying to establish a second connection with Democratic Headquarters. He failed. I know he was frustrated because although I never heard Jim swear, that afternoon, after spending so much time with his ear to the set without a response, he sat back in his chair, let out a long breath, and said, "Damn."

I looked at him and queried, "No luck?"

He replied, "No." Just a very drawn out "no."

He shut the machine off, unplugged the earphones; he put the cover back on it, set it down on the floor adjacent to the table where he had set it up – it was the round table, the table we usually used to eat on.

"We're going to have to make another entry to get this unit that's not working to function properly."

I said to him, "What seems to be the problem? Is it something electronic that is interfering? Is it the placement?"

He looked at me and he said, "I've got to establish exactly where O'Brien's office is located."

I thought that was very odd because there had been at least two entries and it seemed to me that the Democratic National Chairman's office should be easily identifiable. Knowing political operators, there surely had to be a photo array with fellow politicians displayed in a conspicuous manner.

I kept that thought to myself, and said, "John Bailey, the Democrat Chair of the Party in Connecticut was National Chair before O'Brien. Why don't I go into the Headquarters, pose as his nephew going to law school at Georgetown and maybe get a tour of the place—maybe even look around O'Brien's office."

James did not reject the idea out of hand but said, "Let me think about it."

For the next couple of days, we monitored morning, noon, and into the evening as long as anyone was in the Democrat offices. James came every day, sometimes to stay for a while, but always to pick up the notes I typed on the conversations. I typed these notes on paper James had supplied that had carbon and onionskin attached. I am not sure whether the sets he provided had one or two onionskin sheets.

Without fail, James would review the typed pages and highlight certain passages. I do not know if G. Gordon Liddy was given all the transcripts, but I did read in his book that he did not feel there was any useful information in the pages he saw. I know that McCord claimed the surveillance was delivering important material.

There was only one day that McCord failed to pick up the log. He told me he had to go to Miami, and he would call and give me instructions as to what to do with the transcript. He did call, and he instructed me to retain the copy or copies for him but to take the original front page of the log to the Committee to Re-elect the President offices in a sealed envelope marked to the attention of …. and he said the name which was quite unusual. I asked him to spell it and he did. I thought it was a surname, but then he said that was his first name and he gave me the last name—also unusual. I asked him to spell that and he did, and I wrote the name down on the manila envelope in which I put the transcript. The name was so foreign to me that I wasn't sure I got it right, but I wrote it down to the best of my ability and did not ask James to repeat it. I had learned early on that McCord was not used to being asked to repeat himself.

James did ask me to give him the gist of the day's conversations. It had not been a heavy day and I was able to share what I had heard with him.

By the time everyone was gone from Democratic Headquarters and I had cleaned up and changed clothes to go out, it was perhaps nine thirty in the evening. I took the day's transcript to 1701 Pennsylvania Avenue and the offices of the CRP. There was no one around, the front office was locked, but there was a guard. I recognized him as one of ours by his uniform and he asked me what my business was.

I said, "I work for the security department and I am to deliver this package to ..." and I said, "I'm not sure if I can pronounce his name correctly," and I showed him the name on the envelope.

The guard took the envelope and said, "I'll make sure he gets his package."

I said, "Thank you," and I left. I wasn't worried about handing the envelope to the guard—it was a sealed package. The man's name was on it and I trusted that the guard would effect delivery.

At the Watergate burglar's trial, Judge Sirica presiding, for the life of me I could not come up with the man's name nor did I know for certain if he was associated with the CRP or the White House. Sirica insisted that I was deliberately withholding the name of someone associated with the White House. This was not the case. Even when shown a list of possibilities, nothing refreshed my memory.

Author's note: Could the name have been Tony Ulasewicz? A former New York City detective, he was hired in 1969 to unearth negative information about Nixon's enemies. He was the bagman who delivered the cash that was hush money to the Watergate burglars.

One day after James had returned from Miami—of course, I cannot say for sure he was in Miami—but one day after he absented himself from the Howard Johnson—I believe it was on the following Monday or Tuesday, McCord was in Room 723 doing some paperwork when, without preamble, he turned to me and said, "This will be a good time to take your tour."

I changed clothes to look like a law student, walked across the street and presented myself at the receptionist's desk of the Democratic National Headquarters. I said I was John Bailey's nephew; I was at school at Georgetown and I was just curious about where my uncle's office had been.

She said to me, "His secretary is still working here, she's now Mr. O'Brien's secretary, let me call her."

She made her call and soon this woman entered the reception area and I repeated my interest in Chairman Bailey's old office. She was most accommodating and said she would be happy to show me. On the way, she pointed out Spencer Oliver's office and as we went down the hallway, she gave me the names of the people assigned to the various offices.

At the end of the corridor was her office and then we turned right toward the river side of the building and the office of Lawrence O'Brien. She said it had been Bailey's office and there was no problem with my going in as the current Chairman was already in Miami preparing for the Democrat Convention and that he was not scheduled to return before mid-July.

We entered the office. It was magnificent. There were bookcases and all kinds of pictures and citations and awards and paraphernalia on the wall, all with O'Brien's name, of course. She invited me to admire the view from his windows: there was the Potomac River, the White House, the Washington Monument, the 14th Street Bridge, and downtown D.C.

I'm standing there taking it all in while mentally photographing the layout. O'Brien's office was situated on the river side corner of the building. I had to wonder, though, how anyone who had come into the Committee's offices could have missed this office. If it had been "bugged" surely the person who did it—was it McCord?—would have known immediately whose office it was. To this day, I do not know if a device had actually been placed there within construction sections blocking the signal.

I thanked the woman for the tour and went straight across the street to draw a detailed sketch of the L-shaped floorplan while it was fresh in my mind. McCord watched me do it. When I had finished, he took it, went to the telephone, called somebody, I do not know who, and he told whoever it was that he had a sketch of the headquarters and knew exactly what had to be done.

The circumstances surrounding my covert inspection of Democratic National Headquarters have continued to this day to mystify me. The layout was not so complicated that it could not have been easily reproduced by memory by anyone who had entered.

After I had drawn the layout of DNC, I suggested to McCord that, based on the information given to me by the secretary, there was no point in reentering the premises to fix the problem of the malfunctioning device in the Chairman's office. He would not return from the Democratic National Convention in Miami Beach until mid-July and when he did return, he would not be the focus of opposition research. The candidate that the convention picked would be. Still, McCord would be insistent that the team go in the night of June 16–17. There was every reason to abort that night's break-in plan: Among several harbingers of disaster, the burglars had to wait for the last worker to leave at an unusually late hour. The famous taped door had been discovered. But James McCord would not give up. It had to be that night.

Based on the above, I cannot find a logical answer as to why James McCord, who knew all this, insisted on proceeding with the entry to the DNC on the 16th/17th of June. There had to be an alternative motive.

In hindsight, more pieces to the puzzle were added to the big picture.

Then there was the question of his having placed the electronic device on the telephone shared by R. Spencer Oliver and Maxine Wells in the earlier entry. McCord said, "I had an extra one in my pocket so I used it."

That just is not the Jim McCord I knew. The Jim McCord I knew was thorough; he was always precise and everything he did was well planned.

Here is a man who was a former FBI agent, a former CIA agent of the highest trust. He does not act on a whim.

I have the strongest belief that Jim McCord had a specific plan and part of that plan was the Watergate break-in. He had his reasons for his movements that night and he had justification for his later insistence that "the CIA" was not involved. Knowing Jim McCord the way I came to know him by spending so many hours with him in the confines of a hotel room, when he says the CIA was not involved, he is saying the CIA organization as a whole was not involved. It was not a normal operation wherein the various branches of the organization are brought together in the pursuit of its overall agenda. He is not ruling out the possibility that some individuals employed by the CIA then and in the past, individuals who might have had their own reasons for aiding Jim McCord on a mission, were not associated with him to accomplish a certain end.

It is my firm belief that Jim McCord, familiar with all aspects of the CIA and its mission, had the opportunity to use the facilities of the agency to help him and those within the CIA who assisted him in the plot to bring down the president. I truly believe Jim was very comfortable when asked if the CIA was involved to reply, "I will state that the CIA had nothing to do with this operation," without a qualm that he was being truthful. In Jim McCord's mind, he differentiates between the entire CIA and specific individuals, individuals like Richard Helms. The ties between Jim McCord, Richard Helms, and Allen Dulles went back many, many years, and no doubt Helms and Dulles brought Jim McCord from the FBI to the CIA.

It would be contrary to common sense to deny that Dulles, Helms, and McCord did not form friendships when they crossed paths in the intelligence network that existed in Europe during and after the war years of the forties. Dulles became Deputy Director of the CIA in 1951, the same year McCord left the FBI for the CIA. Helms was Director of the intelligence agency when McCord was in charge of security at its headquarters.

And Jim McCord, as noted before, was not just an electronic expert. Everybody who was asked about Jim McCord has agreed with that. He was also a Lieutenant Colonel in the U.S. Air Force and that rank itself testifies to the capabilities of the man. He is not just an airman or just an investigator or just an electronic expert; he had the character and he had the life experiences that led to the part he played in Watergate.

And I truly, truly believe when it became known that Nixon was doing everything in his power to open trade negotiations with the Chinese after having been successful with the Russians, the price he would have to pay became a matter of deep concern in certain quarters.

10

THE BREAK-IN

O n the Wednesday of the second week in June, I let James know I hoped to drive home to Connecticut over the following weekend as my friend, Bob Mirto, had something going in which I was to participate.

He asked if the plan to go to Connecticut could be postponed as he had scheduled work over that weekend beginning on Friday, the 16th of June.

He said, "I'd really like you to stay and be part of what we're doing," and, of course, I agreed.

James remained for several more minutes. There wasn't any activity at the DNC offices so James took a seat and began talking about the incident of the Daniel Ellsberg's office break-in. He wanted to know if I knew anything about it. I responded that all I knew was what I had read in newspaper and magazine articles. James said, "Too bad, it was totally unprofessional." After a few seconds of silence, he said, "Idiots." I didn't question his comment or ask "Who?" We just sat there in silence for a few moments before he said, "We'll have a busy weekend," and he stood and walked toward the door, adding, "Get some rest."

That Friday started off as a normal every-day monitoring day. James didn't show up in the morning, but came in about 4:30 p.m. He seemed the same calm, focused individual I had come to know. He was dressed in a suit as always and was carrying an attache' case. I remember thinking he might be bringing in electronic accessories.

He put the case on my bed and picked up the transcripts I had typed that day. As he glanced over the log, he said, "We're going to be working late tonight," and I said, "Should I change. Are we going out?" and he told me, "No, you'll be staying here. Stay casual."

He sat down as Jim would do, opened his briefcase, took out a sheaf of papers, looked across the street at the lights on in Democratic Headquarters, and asked, "How long has that person been over there?"

I said, "Been there all day."

He was sitting with his back toward the street, so he said, "Let me know when they leave."

He sat there for several minutes, and I saw him glancing over to Democratic Headquarters and the look on his face combined with his attitude told me he was troubled. Then he started to talk to me. There were several times when he paused, and I could have commented but something made me hesitate. He had something to say and he said it, and somehow I knew he wanted me to remember it. Between the lines, I thought he was saying "Now, Al, I want you to remember this. I don't want you to forget what I'm saying."

I know he talked about the cost in human lives of Nixon's dealing with the Russians. He even mentioned a number. And then he said, "This trip to China. Not a good idea." I was thinking what the hell are you talking about.

I didn't know about any trip to China.[3] Maybe I should have read about it in the paper or in Newsweek but I had not. The only thing I knew anything about was Russia. Russia was on the agenda.

Some time passed and we're approaching ten o'clock when he turned and asked, "There're still there?" and I said, "Yeah," and he said, "Wow," he just went, "Wow."

He got up, walked over to pick up the telephone, called someone and reported, "We've got somebody really dedicated over there—there're still working." Then came a pause on his end before he said, "No, I don't think we should cancel. Give it another hour."

He hung up the phone. He walked over, and he stood in the doorway to the balcony that looked over the street and he said, "I don't know how long this person is going to work but I don't want to cancel."

Now I realize there's going to be an entry across the street. For the first time I found myself wondering if this entry would be illegal.

I had given some thought to whether or not the interception of telephone conversations we were doing was legal. I had come to the conclusion, based on my legal experience, that what we were doing could not be illegal since Attorney General John Mitchell, the highest legal officer in the country, was aware of it and had been involved in the decision to do what we were doing. I never gave any thought of justifying what we were doing on the basis of national security. I just relied on the involvement of John Mitchell. I put against my qualms that Jim McCord had given me a full report on a meeting chaired by then Attorney General John Mitchell he had attended in which the electronic surveillance had been discussed.

Finally, the lights went out across the street. Both McCord and I observed the individual going through the reception area and out the doors.

---

3 President Richard Nixon had astounded the world by making a trip to Communist China in February of 1972.

We could see that he stopped outside the door and locked it. We could see him go toward the elevator. This was after midnight in the early morning hours of Saturday, June 17, 1972.[4]

McCord went to the phone, called someone and said, "He's left. The place is empty," then listened for a few minutes before adding, "O.K."

With that, Jim moved from the bedside table that held the phone and a lamp, halfway down the length of the bed where he stopped and very deliberately removed his watch and placed it on the bedspread. Then he took his wallet and some keys out of his pocket and put them, too, on the bed. I believe he also removed a ring as well. In other words, he removed everything from his person that might have revealed his identity.

Next, he reached in the pocket of his suit coat and took out a walkie-talkie radio, a small hand-sized model. I do not know whether it was government issued or commercial. He said, "You know how to use this?" and I said, "Basically," and he gave me a brief five-minute tutorial on its use.

Then he went over and turned on the television.

One of the Washington police officers would later claim that I neglected my watchman duties because I was engrossed in a movie on TV entitled The Attack of the Puppet People. *That is simply a blatant fabrication. McCord himself turned on the TV and adjusted the volume so that if you were outside the door to the room any communication inside the room would be disguised. He did not select or change a channel. Whatever channel to which the TV was tuned remained selected. He changed nothing except the volume and this he adjusted to a low level suited to the early morning hour. I know McCord wanted to ensure that no one in the hallway could hear anything going on in the room.*

---

4 Later revealed as Bruce Givner, a UCLA government intern taking advantage of the W.A.T.S line to talk to friends and family around the nation.

McCord gave me instructions: I was to pay specific attention to the sixth floor across the street. If any lights came on any other floor to immediately notify him and he then said, "Let's test the unit."

With James at one end of the room and me at the other, we then went through a brief routine of testing of his unit and my unit. We agreed that I would use the call signal, "Base" after other call signs were rejected.

When he was satisfied that the units were working, he stood in the doorway of our balcony and he looked across at the Democratic National Headquarters. All was still dark. No lights had reappeared. We were well into the early morning hours of June 17, that infamous Saturday morning that changed my life and the history of our country.

James walked to the door, put his hand on the doorknob, turned to me and said, "Take care." Never had he said anything like that to me before. "Take care," he said, and he said it very seriously. Those words and the way he said them have never left my mind to this day.

And then he was gone.

I made sure all the lights in the room were out and then I stepped out onto the balcony. I had on a white shirt and I kind of wondered if I were visible to anyone looking over at the Howard Johnson, but the only light behind me was from the TV.

I just stood there and within a few moments Jim appeared on the street below coming from the Howard Johnson garage. I saw him cross the street. There was no one else in sight. He proceeded down the driveway leading into the Watergate complex underground garage. He stopped, turned, and I know he looked back in my direction. I was about halfway out on the balcony. I'm not sure if he could see me so I stepped forward toward the parapet but by that time he had disappeared into the maw of the garage.

Regarding the entry into the DNC offices that night, I would like to add one thing: regardless of what has been previously written, James McCord, being the perfectionist he was, would not have assigned or allowed anyone *else to tape open the doors that were taped the way they were taped. The tap-ing was obviously deliberately done in such a way by someone who wanted the tape to be discovered. Without doubt, McCord was the leader on the 16—17 June. He was the individual who made the decision whether to abort or go forward. He determined when the entry would take place. He would not have delegated the taping of the lock to permit opening the door to someone else. The taping of the door to the underground garage at Watergate was discov-ered by the Watergate guard, Frank Wills. Wills removed the tape thinking that maintenance or a guest wanting to unload luggage had taped it open and forgot to remove it. On a later round, Wills found the door re-taped. Would an experienced spook take the risk of putting on a second tape when the first had been spotted? This was a well-planned act that had to be discovered, and it was.*

Another piece to the puzzle is now in place.

I do not know how much time elapsed before I saw lights on the eighth floor across the street, two floors above the Democratic National Headquarters. The lights went on and I pushed the button on my radio and said: "Base to any unit—we have lights on the eighth floor."

Soon those lights went off and lights came on on the seventh floor, the floor directly above Democratic Headquarters. "Base to any unit we have lights on the seventh floor," I warned. I would say the time was then approx-imately 2:00 a.m.

A voice came back. It was not Jim McCord's. The voice said, "No prob-lem, that's the guard check."

I did not respond. I continued to watch. I didn't see lights go on on the sixth or any other floor.

Perhaps five minutes later I observed this rather old, four-door sedan, it could have been a Ford or a Chevy, pull up in front of the Watergate complex. Three men, dressed in clothes that matched the dilapidated vehicle, moved up the steps to the main entrance of the Watergate complex. One of them tried the door and it was obviously locked.

As I later learned, when the call came in to the dispatcher about suspicious activity at the Watergate complex, the uniformed police officer on duty had parked his squad car and allegedly gone into a bar. The three off-duty undercover officers had been for some time unaccountably loitering in a nondescript automobile just two blocks from the Watergate complex. They heard the call; one of them told the dispatcher they would respond. This suspicious coincidence would raise significant skepticism in the investigation of Watergate.

As I watched, a guard came to the door and one of the newcomers held his hand up in the manner I recognized as showing an identification.

I got immediately on the radio and said, "Base to any unit. We have three individuals just entered the building."

A voice came back and said, "What have you got?"

I said, "We have three individuals dressed casually, hippie type individuals in the building. We've got lights going on on the top floor. I can't see movement."

I did not get a reply.

Almost immediately, the lights came on throughout the sixth floor, I saw movement in Ida Wells' office. Suddenly the door to the balcony opened and two individuals, both brandishing guns, began a search of this outside area.

I learned later that they also observed me and initially wondered if I had anything to do with the unfolding events. Agreeing that I was probably just someone getting some night air, they continued searching. While they were on the balcony, I again used the walkie-talkie to advise anyone listening about their activity. I said, "We've got people outside. They've got guns. Are our people in suits or casual?"

A voice replied, "Suits. Why?"

I said, "We've got a problem. They're in casual and they've got guns."

Before there was any reply, the men on the balcony turned and went back inside.

While the two were on the balcony, another individual entered the office space, and I saw him looking under the desk with a flashlight. Then he disappeared.

Shortly after that, I heard, "They've got us." And then, there is this voice and there is no doubt in my mind it was Jim McCord because I know his voice well. He said "Are you Metro police?" I will never forget it. I can hear those words in my mind to this day.

Regarding the words "Are you metro police?" only one of the five men that night knew to refer to Washington police by the term "metro." That was McCord. Those words were precisely spoken by a very precise man and translated to "mission accomplished."

Then one after another, police squad cars began to pull up in the area in front of the Watergate and I was back on the air and I was saying, "Base to any unit. We've got all kinds of police vehicles arriving. Different police officers arriving, uniform police, bicycle police, we've got everybody."

A voice came back, not McCord's, "Stay put, I'll be right over."

I'm standing on the balcony and I observe two men coming out on the driveway to the garage area underneath the Watergate complex. I continue to focus on the police activity over at the Watergate offices.

In just a matter of a few minutes the door to the room opens. It wasn't locked. I kept the door open for McCord to come and go.

This gentleman came in and I recognized him as one of the individuals I had been introduced to a couple of weeks before. I later learnt he was E. Howard Hunt.

He hurried in and the first thing he said was, "I've got to use the bathroom," and he went in there and closed the door. The lights were not on in the room.

In a few minutes, he came out and said, "Where's your phone?" and I pointed toward the bedside table.

He proceeded to make a phone call and I gathered he was advising whomever was on the other end to get somebody down to the police station to determine what the police were going to do, and he discussed the possible necessity to get them attorneys. I paid little attention to his conversation as my attention still centered on what was taking place over at the Watergate.

After he hung up the telephone, he looked around and he said, "Wipe this room down. Pack up everything. Get it the hell out of here."

I asked, "Take it where?"

"McCord's house," he said, and then, "I don't care if you throw it in the river. Just get it the hell out of here."

He turned then and walked hastily toward the door.

He was out the door. I had been looking forward to being part of the security force at the Republican National Convention in Florida in July with some excitement.

I followed Hunt partway down the hallway.

I yelled after him, "Does this mean I'm not going to Miami?"

He stopped and looked back. He didn't say anything. He just gave me a look of disgust and headed for the elevators.

I turned back into the room and I thought, "God, I've been living here for two weeks, there's no way I can thoroughly wipe this room down. Besides I've charged phone calls to my family to this room. To hell with it."

I opened Jim McCord's briefcase to put the personal items he had removed from his person into it. To my surprise, in the bottom of the case under some other items was a set of onionskin copies of the logs I had typed.

Here they were, the Gemstone Files, in Jim McCord's briefcase. I thought, "What in the hell are they doing here?"

There was also a large quantity of hundred-dollar bills loose and there were some still in bank paper binders. I don't know how many were in each packet.

I placed all his personal items into his briefcase. I packed up all the equipment into their cases, then went downstairs and commandeered one of those large baggage carts, loaded everything in the room on to the cart, and took it down to the garage where James kept a van. The key to that van stayed in the room so I was able to use it to drive to the McCord house in Rockville, Maryland.

I awakened Mrs. McCord and she drove me back to the Howard Johnson. She did not dress, she made the trip in her nightgown and bathrobe. Enroute, I told her what had happened as far as I knew. She might have been a little teary, but she concealed her emotions well. She was calm. She listened to what I had to say. She did not ask any questions. She did not even ask if I knew where he had been taken.

When we arrived back at the Howard Johnson garage, I thanked her, got into my personal car that James had insisted so recently that I bring to Washington. I had packed my personal belongings into the vehicle at the same time I was packing the van.

11

ESCAPE TO CONNECTICUT

T he normal six-hour drive between D.C. and Connecticut took only three hours. I could not understand the lack of police presence within those East Coast states that allowed me to violate every state's maximum speed limit and other applicable motor vehicle statutes such as reckless driving, etc.—but I was grateful for it.

Arriving in my home area at approximately 8:30 a.m., I decided to head to the residence of a good friend, Walter Walsh, in Hamden, Connecticut, and use his phone. I did not want to venture to my own residence in case the FBI or some other law enforcement agency would be there.

Walter's mother met me at the door; Walter was still sleeping. She invited me to have breakfast, but I was in no state to enjoy it. She graciously led me to the telephone, and I dialed the home number of Robert Mirto, attorney and best friend, whose law office was in nearby West Haven, Connecticut. When Bob answered I told him I had to see him immediately, that I needed to engage him as my lawyer, and I began to tell him the nature of the events of the last twenty-hours hours.

When I hung up and turned to leave, I found that unbeknownst to me, Walter had awakened and was standing behind me. After asking him a few questions, I realized he had heard enough to know its importance and my involvement.

I had to take several minutes to obtain from him his oath that if he heard or read anything related to my conversation, his lips would be sealed. It took several minutes, but finally he said, "No one will be able to make me talk. I'll die protecting you."

Well, Walter's oath was good for some ten days when he was interviewed by the FBI and his chance "to die protecting me" occurred. Although he initially refused to cooperate, as soon as the interviewing agents mentioned "aiding and abetting a criminal," he told them everything including some unrelated antics. Despite his talking to the FBI, we remained close friends. In later years, his "rolling over" became a good story and was the source of merriment.

When I called Robert Mirto that Saturday morning, June 17, we arranged to meet at his office, some twenty minutes away. When I arrived, I found that he had recently taken on a partner, John Cassidento, an attorney we both knew who had left his position as a federal prosecutor with the United States attorney's office in New Haven, Connecticut, to join Mirto's law firm. John wanted to become a judge and was taking the necessary steps to obtain an appointment in the Connecticut court system.

Later, when Cassidento became a judge, articles on his achievements included the fact that he had represented two famous clients, Sonny Metz, a union leader who was an alleged Mafia associate, and Al Baldwin, who was involved with Watergate. What Bob and I did not know on that June morning in Bob's office was that Cassidento had another client—Larry O'Brien and his Democratic Party.

I sat down with Bob and John, and, over a few hours, related the facts of my personal involvement in what had taken place. I engaged them to represent me in any legal repercussions I would face. We then arranged to meet the following Monday to answer further questions they had.

I went to my own home in North Haven and waited for the inevitable contact from the local police or the FBI, but none came. I returned to Mirto's office on Monday, the 19th of June, briefed them on details I had remembered in the meantime and answered their further questions. They also learned about the very important information that I had knowledge that pointed to the involvement of John Mitchell, the Attorney General, in the Watergate affair.

Bob and I were completely in the dark as to John Cassidento's moves immediately after my first interview with the two attorneys. Probably on Sunday, but it could have been in the middle of the following week, John Cassidento went to Washington, met with Larry O'Brian, the Chairman of the Democratic National Committee, and others, and revealed everything I had related. This shocking betrayal of friendship, lawyer/client privilege, and ethics in pursuit of a judgeship gave the Democrats, at an early date, details they might never have learned. They had, from Cassidento, enough solid information to file a lawsuit against the Committee to Re-elect the President and on or about June 25, 1972, filed charges that would prove to be the opening of the crescendo that would build to finally remove a president.

(It was not until twenty years after the events that Mirto and Baldwin discovered Cassidento had immediately divulged Baldwin's account to Democratic attorneys. Cassidento's role was revealed in an article in the *Washington Post* on June 28, 1992.)

Either on Tuesday, the 20th, or Wednesday, the 21st, Paul O'Brien, the attorney for the CRP, journeyed from Washington to consult with Mirto. He was most unhappy to learn that Baldwin claimed to have information connecting John Mitchell with the burglary.

Mirto asked O'Brien for the names of any services of a Washington, D.C., lawyer who could represent his client in any legal action that would take place in the District of Columbia. His response was that since Alfred Baldwin never worked for the CRP, but rather had worked for McCord Associates, a private firm, neither the Committee nor their legal representatives had any obligation to him.

O'Brien had said, Bob reported to Al, "You're nothing but a sheet blowing in the wind."

Mirto said, "You're on your own, Al, and we have to do whatever we have to do to protect you." And Al said, "All right—whatever develops let me know."

Al related for the tape:

Of course, all this my lawyers told me later and I knew nothing of O'Brien's position then. I was seated in the reception area while Mirto and O'Brien were closeted in Bob's office. At some point while I was waiting there to talk to Bob myself, O'Brien exited my lawyer's private office and walked toward the rear exit that led to the parking lot in the back of the building.

O'Brien glanced back into the waiting room and suddenly turned on his heel and came directly at me in an obviously aggressive manner. Without preamble, without confirming who I was, he delivered a threat: "When we get through with you, you won't even be able to get a job driving a truck."

I was to learn just how effective whomever he represented would be in sabotaging my attempts to find employment after the Watergate trials and hearings were over.

Bob Mirto later said that their decision to cut me loose "was the worst mistake they made." When some of the Cuban participants complained to James McCord about what they considered my treachery, he defended me by pointing out that I had first gone for help to the Committee to no avail.

In the meantime, the news of the break-in was all over the media and Baldwin was expecting the law to knock on his door at any time. The attempted burglary of Democratic National Headquarters in Washington,

D.C., was not then limited to investigation as a local crime by local police. The FBI had become involved.

L. Patrick Gray, the temporary director of the FBI, had received information that led to the Bureau's joining the hunt. Gray had been considered an unusual appointment. Nixon had passed over all the assistant directors at the FBI and chosen this Naval officer. Gray assigned Angelo Lanno, of the Washington field office, to the case.

Al Baldwin's listening post at HoJo's was quickly discovered by the FBI. Bureau agents were anxious to interview him. Federal prosecutors were threatening to file charges. Both attorneys—Mirto and Cassidento—made trips to Washington on his behalf.

I have to interject here Baldwin's conviction that Mark Felt was not Deep Throat. It is important to this account because the Woodward–Bernstein team knew nothing of Baldwin's existence until other media broke the story.

The ex-FBI agent offers this take:

Mark Felt's career at the FBI was marked by huge promotions. I actually looked at some of his fitness reports on an FBI channel, and I was astounded at the glowing reviews of his prowess. It was widely believed that Felt had accomplished such leaps in the chain of command because everybody wanted to get rid of him.

Felt, however, believed the flattering reviews. He assumed he was going to get Hoover's job and one reason he didn't was because he was so universally disliked.

As assistant director at the Bureau in June and July of 1972, he would have had knowledge of the involvement of Al Baldwin and access to the interviews of Al Baldwin by the Washington FBI agents. He could have accessed their FBI 302s which contained pertinent information including Attorney General John Mitchell's connection to the break-in. Mitchell's involvement while still occupying the high office of attorney general would have been a huge news story in the early days after the Watergate arrests. Deep Throat never provided Woodward and Bernstein with this information. Instead, the team was directed by Deep Throat to the narrow path of "Follow the money."

I do not know when Felt's mental acuity began to fail, but when he appeared in the doorway of his home and was captured by the cameras waving to the crowd of news reporters, it was very obvious he was suffering severe old-age memory loss and delusion. I would venture to say that Bob Woodward, his supposed contact during the Watergate investigations, recognized that this pathetic attempt for fame was the perfect cover to conceal the real Deep Throat's identity.

It is important to remember that in 1972, Mark Felt, then an Assistant Director at the FBI, had not succeeded to the throne. It had been Felt's lifelong aspiration to replace Hoover. Felt's dream was shattered by reality. President Nixon refused to appoint him to the directorship. That bitter disappointment gave Felt every reason to use FBI resources, if available, to embarrass or discredit Nixon.

Hence, it follows that had he known about Baldwin, the real Deep Throat surely would have passed the information to the reporters that there was someone who could put John Mitchell in the picture. That he did not is evident from the fact that it was not until an interview in the *Los Angeles Times* was published that the Washington Post learned of the existence of witness Al Baldwin.

The *Los Angeles Times* published an extensive interview with Al Baldwin on October 10, 1972. Reporter Jack Nelson was the author of this front-page article. The stir from its publication caused Ben Bradlee, editor of the *Washington Post*, the newspaper that was leading the hunt for Nixon as the ultimate villain of the conspiracy, to set his lead dogs Woodward and Bernstein on Al Baldwin.

Thus, a very important fact is that the FBI knew of Baldwin's participation in the Watergate burglary from June 1972 to October of 1972, yet
Deep Throat never alerted Woodward to that information.

When Woodward belatedly contacted Baldwin's attorneys,
Cassidento put a price for access to him that was prohibitively high, and
Woodward abandoned his pursuit of such a session. At the time, John
Cassidento claimed his demand was a deliberate ploy to discourage the
Washington Post investigative team from further contact. Hindsight forces
one to wonder if John had some ulterior motive. Even Bob Mirto was sur-
prised at his partner's action, but the outcome was that Woodward never
made another approach.

But, back to the story of Al Baldwin's looming legal troubles:

*The United States attorney's office contacted my attorneys and John
Cassidento accompanied me on my first trip back to Washington after the
Watergate arrests of June 17. In spite of his surreptitious visit to Washington
to tell all, I cannot fault John's representation of my interests in the face of Earl
Silbert's threats. He never faulted in pursuing the goal he and Bob Mirto had
set—they would extract for me a promise not to prosecute. Immunity was not
an option.*

*They definitely did not want me to have to testify before a Grand Jury
because once you go before a Grand Jury, it is like opening the floodgates
allowing all kinds of charges to be leveled against you.*

*That was the mindset with which Cassidento and I entered the office of
Assistant United States Attorney for the District of Columbia, Earl Silbert, the
lead prosecutor for the government preparing to try the Watergate culprits.*

*Inside the room, in addition to Silbert's assistants, were at least eleven
individuals, all male and all in suits. A pair of them were standing adjacent
to the doorway through which we entered, another pair stood next to the desk
while the others stood in strategic locations around the room.*

Mr. Silbert rose, introduced himself, and extended his hand to John and then to me. He then introduced his two assistants before sitting back down. I realized the other men in the room were not to be introduced and quickly concluded they were FBI agents. I believe among them was Angelo Lanno.

I felt sure that they were there to arrest me if I did not cooperate.

John leaned over and whispered, "You know who those guys are?" and I said, "Yes, they are agents," and he said, "Yes, they are."

Silbert wasted no time and told John exactly what he expected from me in words to the effect that "Mr. Baldwin is not going to walk out of this office today. He's not going to walk out of here a free man. He's either going to cooperate or he will pay the consequences."

There was no doubt in my mind that his "consequences" were that I would be placed under arrest. My assessment was based on my FBI experience of what was going on and I think John, having been an Assistant United States Attorney in New Haven, Connecticut, had come to the same conclusion.

What was interesting to me was the wording Silbert used when he first addressed the two of us. He had said, "John, I know you are a former Assistant U.S. Attorney, so I am not going to cushion my words."

John Cassidento leaned forward when Silbert ended this statement and pointing directly at Silbert, he said, "It's very easy to indict. You can indict Donald Duck, Mickey Mouse, and Pluto. Convicting them is another matter. And you're not going to convict Al Baldwin of anything."

I sat there in total disbelief, thinking, "My God, John, what the hell are you doing?" but before I could form another thought, I felt John's hand on my arm pulling me up from my seat.

I was thinking, "What is going on here? These are guys you don't want to mess with."

But John was adamant. "Come on, Al. Let's go," and he stood up and he looked at the two agents standing near Mr. Silbert in front of a pair of

*windows looking out on the local scene and I waited just a few seconds to see
if they were going to make a move to stop me before I stood up and I looked
at the other two agents who were standing by the door and John said, "Follow
me," and he started walking toward the door and the two men moved aside.*

*John turned from the door and said to Silbert: "We're out of here, when
you get serious, call me."*

*John opened the door and we were greeted by dozens of reporters and I
remember the first person I recognized was a young Lesley Stahl. I think she
was with CBS and she said, "Mr. Baldwin, would you give an interview?" and
she handed me her business card and she said, "Please consider contacting
us," and I said, "I'll give this to my attorney," and the two of us walked out and
we returned to Connecticut.*

*I was behind the wheel on the way home and I remember John deliv-
ering a dissertation on the tactics of the U.S. attorney's office and his analogy
of it being like a chess game. Not being a chess player, I was relieved when he
went to sleep for the rest of the drive.*

By the time Cassidento and Baldwin returned to Connecticut, Mirto
had been contacted by Earl Silbert who wanted Baldwin back in D.C. the
following day.

As indicated, Mirto's goal was to protect his client and friend from
appearing before the Grand Jury and to wrest from the United States
Attorney a promise not to prosecute. From his experience, Mirto feared
a Grand Jury appearance would no doubt result in some charge even if
it were not the initial charge threatened. Toward this end, Mirto took his
client to Washington to visit Earl Silbert once again. Al remembers this
about the trip:

*Bob wanted to determine how the United States attorney was planning
to handle me. Was I to be indicted? Was I to be a witness? Was I going to be
given immunity?*

When we arrived at Silbert's office, we found two FBI agents in the room and I remember Silbert saying to Mirto: "The first thing I want from him is for him to sit down with the FBI agents and lay out what he knows, and then I want to look at that, and we will see where we go from there."

I remember Bob specifically saying to Earl Silbert: "Al is going to name John Mitchell so that's all you need to know. Let's have a decision today. We're down here from Connecticut. We're not going to stay overnight, we're heading back. Let's have a decision today," and Silbert came back with, "Let me think about it. Come back," and he looked at his watch—this was like eleven o'clock—and he said, "Be back here at two o'clock," and we left.

We didn't go to lunch as I expected. Instead, Bob said we were going to the office of Paul O'Brien, a partner in one of the premier law firms in D.C. with an unmatched reputation for the practice of law and for their political connections. As stated before, O'Brien had been retained by CRP to represent them in defending the suit filed by the Democratic National Committee.

We had no appointment, but Bob told the receptionist he was Attorney Robert Mirto from Connecticut with his client Alfred Baldwin, and then he said, "I'd like to talk to Mr. O'Brien, but Mr. Baldwin will not be coming in with me."

The receptionist turned her back and spoke very softly into the telephone before turning our way and saying, "He'll see you now—I've got a secretary coming to show you to his office." Almost immediately the escort appeared, and Bob disappeared through an interior door.

I took a seat in the plush surroundings tastefully and expensively furnished. A few minutes passed before Bob returned and when we were walking out, he said to me: "They've certainly left you blowing in the wind. Their position is that you never worked for the Committee to Re-elect the President. They have searched and there is no record of your employment. O'Brien wants nothing to do with you. We are of no significance to the Committee to Re-elect."

I assume my employment records had been shredded along with the other reams of material that were disposed of in the cover-up once the facts of the burglary had been published and the identity of McCord as the Committee's security chief and his ties to the CIA revealed.

As we walked along, Bob asked: "What have you got that shows you worked for the Committee to Re-elect the President? I said, "I have two checks I haven't cashed with the attachment that identifies the payer as CRP along with the checking account routing number and the account number which can be tracked. "

We walked a few more steps and I remembered, "I have my security pin." CRP's security pins were identifiable but were enough like the Secret Service pins that if you went to the White House, they'd wave you through.

There's something else I recalled as we walked—it might have been that I had made a copy of the form I completed the day I was hired.

The proof may not have been good enough for CRP's hotshot attorney, but it was good enough that I subsequently won a federal lawsuit filed against the Committee to Re-elect the President.

Eventually, United States Attorney Silbert agreed that we would have a promise not to prosecute and that opened the door for the FBI to begin their interrogation as to my part in the whole affair, a grueling experience over the span of two days. Special Agent Angelo Lanno was the lead FBI agent investigating my involvement assisted by Agent Daniel Mayham.

I do want to interject here that I believe the focus of the interviews conducted with me followed a certain preconceived approach. As a former agent, I was schooled in interrogation technique, and I was not subjected to anything like a far-flung net for reeling in all possible evidence. It was clear to me that they did not want to elicit any explanations or any evidence exonerating any of the accused. There was an air of the political about the investigation that would never have been permitted under J. Edgar Hoover. With all his faults, God help you if, as an agent, you ever acted from a political motive. Politics was not allowed in the FBI in that era. When you look at what's happening today with the FBI, one has to suspect it has become a political Bureau. It is no longer independent.

Once I agreed to cooperate, I was asked many times why I agreed to do so. Several interviewers assumed I agreed to avoid prison. The truth is, I never thought about prison. Prison never entered my mind; being arrested never entered my mind. I cooperated in order to avoid the Grand Jury. That was our whole purpose. Stay away from the Grand Jury. Because once you get in front of the Grand Jury, it is unlikely you will come away unscathed. You will get burned. My attorneys' insistence about that followed advice I learned in law school and it was probably reinforced as I worked as an agent myself. You just have to avoid the Grand Jury. Especially if you feel that you are innocent. Avoid it. You don't want any kind of charge from which you have to defend yourself because the minute the charge is placed against you, 98 percent of the time, you are going to be branded as guilty. If you appear before a Grand Jury and they indict you, you are going to have a tough time in a trial facing a biased jury. Our whole focus was that promise not to prosecute and once I was given that, I cooperated.

12

WITNESS FOR THE PROSECUTION

S oon after I began to cooperate with the FBI, my first session of inter-rogation being June 25, phone contact between James McCord and me began. Initially, James called me from a pay phone and gave me a pay phone number to call. When I did so, he answered. After that, for some time we followed the routine of talking between telephone booths. Jim was con-vinced his home telephone was bugged.

I had not talked to James since his arrest, and prior to his initial con-tact, I experienced no little trepidation about how he was reacting to my cooperation with the FBI. Even as I called that pay phone at his request, I anticipated his expressing disappointment in me, maybe even angry recrimi-nations. Nothing like that occurred. He was as considerate as he always was; there was no recrimination. His attitude during our conversation was "you do what you have to do" and that continued to be his stance through every succeeding interchange.

He asked me a few questions as to what I had told the FBI. For instance, I remember distinctly his asking if I had related the reconnaissance *of McGovern headquarters and I said, "Yes, I did." My answer did not upset him.*

Often during these telephone exchanges, I would express concern for his situation. I might say, "James if I say anything about this or anything about that, it's definitely going to affect you," and he would answer, "You do what you have to do. You need to tell the truth." Dozens of times he insisted on my sticking to the truth. "You need to tell the truth." He kept stressing that to me. "I have no problem with what you're going to do." How could he know what I was going to do? How could he possibly say do what you have to do? In other words, I had to be in a way, quote, set up. There is no doubt in my mind that he knew exactly how I would react.

Over the time I was cooperating, I continued talking to James McCord. From some aspects of our conversations, I realized he knew what was going on with the FBI. Still, at one point, he said, "You do whatever you feel is necessary. Don't hold back." Those words, "Don't hold back," were very telling. James' choice of phrasing always meant something, and I learned to pay attention to that. In one exchange he indicated that he had hired me knowing I would tell the truth and he wanted me to continue to do so. At no time did he ever even hint that I should take a different course of action. At no time did he ever even suggest to me that I should deny anything or alter my account to benefit him. He actually said to me, "I know you are going to tell the truth." How did he know I would tell the truth?

I refer back to my belief that having located me in the roster of the Retired FBI Agents organization in Connecticut, he had taken advantage of his connections at the CIA to have a psychological profile of me constructed so there was no need of his asking me the normal questions one would ask in an interview prior to hiring.

Of this, I have no doubt in my mind whatsoever given the way I was hired without any background check, without any forms being filled out, without any questioning me about my experience.

Why would he? He already knew all the answers.

I just can't see my being given a job in which I would be interacting with White House personnel, prominent Republicans amongst other noteworthy individuals, given a weapon, and being trusted by an intelligence veteran like James McCord, that the only information available to them was my contact data filed with the Retired FBI Agents organization.

Even as late as 1975, I received a letter from James McCord in which he wrote, "I have always been glad that you took the course which you did and that you undertook to tell the truth as you knew it.... The nation, of course, owes you a debt for what you did, and for your own integrity."

The Watergate puzzle has now taken on a recognizable form.

Amazingly, it is dominated by a portrait of James McCord. That likeness should be proudly displayed in the hall of fame room at CIA headquarters in Langley, Virginia, next to Allen Dulles and Richard Helms. Of course, such honor will never be bestowed.

History is now given the task to reevaluate Watergate in light of the new revelations included in the account of what I saw and heard during my personal experience of that political upheaval. My account is largely a portrayal of James McCord's character in conflict with what he perceived as a threat to his country and to the independence of the CIA from political machinations. I am convinced that he played a central role in forcing the resignation of President Richard Milhous Nixon and concluding that he was the constant hero in the whole sometimes sordid, sometimes shameful, sometimes bewildering affair is justified.

Over the next few months, through the series of shockers uncovered by reporters, through trials and hearings, through accusations and denials, through revelations of truth and perjury so entertaining to the public, Jim and I talked many times.

I saw James in person in January of 1973 in the hallway at the Federal Court House during the Federal criminal trial. We shook hands, we said hello, and James said something like, "I have no problem, Al, with your testimony." Again, I got the feeling that he knew what was going on. Maybe he even knew what my testimony would be. "Good luck testifying today," he added.

Whether or not McCord read a transcript of my testimony, I'll never know, but I do know he never expressed any problem or any issues with any of it. "You do what you have to do," seemed to be his theme throughout. So many times, he told me, "Al, I have no problem with what you will say." And he demonstrated that to me in every telephone conversation, every exchange of ideas and information I had with him from the first day to the last contact.

I never felt that I was betraying James. I believe he is just one of several co-conspirators who believed Nixon did the unforgiveable in striking the deal to allow the giants of American industry to go into Soviet territory and open shop. I honestly feel that Jim would be pleased to have the truth come out, to have history set aright. So many times he told me, "Al, I have no problem with the truth."

I did tell James once that someday I would reveal what I believed to be the reason for Watergate, and that my story would be centered around him. I told him, "I'm committed to honoring you, James, if you are all right with that." I told him I would wait until he passed, not because then he could not rebut my account but because I wanted to avoid his having to deal with the media again. I also said, "I'll never say anything until I know for certain it will not affect you or your family."

I discussed this with my attorneys, and they agreed this would be the best course. They did, however, allow one thorough interview to go public— the L. A. Times piece.

There are several factors that indicate to me James McCord never completely severed his relationship with the CIA. Although he would insist that the CIA was not involved in Watergate, I believe the door was always open to Mr. McCord to take advantage of any services the CIA had to offer. The James McCord I knew would never lie and could in good conscience deny that the

CIA was operating in Watergate if only three or four of the old hands from the World War II OSS who were now high up in the CIA were engaged.

If James McCord had his back against the wall and was asked if certain CIA employees had helped him, in my opinion, he would have answered truthfully, that yes, there were certain individuals in certain departments who assisted him while he was employed as Security Director by the Committee to Re-elect the President. There is also the possibility that if the question had been asked, McCord would rely on an old tactic to take the hounds off the scent. He would begin his answer by making an analogy to facts similar but not exactly on point. Then he would provide an answer which, in most instances, would be accepted by his interrogators who are now oblivious to their original question and, thus, one that would not be answered. I have witnessed McCord employing this method.

When McCord wrote that "every tree in the forest will fall," he predicted what happened. I believe by the "forest" he meant the White House and the trees that fell included Ehrlichman, Haldeman, Dean, etc. and the big tree himself, Richard Nixon.

Today, if one listens attentively, one might hear the words echoing throughout the universe of patriotism a "Well done, McCord. Some rotten trees in the forest have fallen including the biggest tree of all while the wide forest continues to flourish."

I am convinced that the entire scandal that forced Nixon to resign was a well-planned operation. I believe Nixon's predilection for untruthfulness had been demonstrated over his career and a CIA psychological profile underscored that trait and predicted how he would try to dodge the repercussions of Watergate.

Another piece to the puzzle slides into place.

13

TRIALS AND HEARINGS

As Baldwin said that it was John Cassidento who gave the Democrats everything they needed to file a lawsuit against the CRP. Prior to his furtive trip from New Haven to Washington to divulge Al's story to Larry O'Brien et al., they had only a page four newspaper article about the break-in. All the information the Democrats had was obtained based on Cassidento's participation in the exchanges between client and attorneys, in Mirto's law office in West Haven, Connecticut, on Monday and Tuesday, June 19 and 20, 1972.

When Cassidento, breaking all legal and moral restraints, began to feed the confidential information Al Baldwin revealed to his attorneys over the two days of concentrated consultation apprising them of the details of his assignments while employed by the CRP, the Democratic Party had more than enough evidence to file the one million dollar lawsuit against the CRP that they instituted on June 21, 1972.

Cassidento's motive for breaking attorney/client privilege was his lust for a judgeship. He did get one but lived only a short time to enjoy the honor.

The HoJo lookout testified in the trial of the Watergate Seven in January, 1973, with Judge John Sirica presiding. He was a key witness in several subsequent proceedings: a civil lawsuit filed by the Democrats against the CREEP, and at the Senate and House Judiciary Committee hearings in 1973–74.

With respect to the criminal trial in January 1973 in Federal Court, there was one issue concerning Baldwin's testimony that annoyed Judge Sirica. McCord had instructed Baldwin to deliver the Gemstone transcript summary of what was heard one particular day in June to an individual at the CRP.

McCord had given his assistant the name of the person who was to receive the transcript. At day's end, Baldwin sealed the transcript in an envelope and at approximately 9:30 p.m. that evening delivered the package to the guard on duty at the CRP office. The guard took the envelope, examined the name of the addressee, which he seemed to recognize, and assured Baldwin he would deliver same to the person.

When questioned by the prosecutor, Al could not recall the name of the receiver of the package. The Judge took over the questioning and called out eight to ten names none of which Al could honestly identify as the name of the man to whom the package was intended. Presuming the witness was deliberately avoiding naming the individual, the Judge called a recess ordering the attorneys to meet with him in chamber. Al was subjected to further hammering.

When court resumed the Judge again read the list and not receiving an affirmative answer to any of them, he allowed the prosecutor to continue his questioning. The criminal trial continued, and history has recorded the verdicts and sentencing imposed by the court.

This kind of aggressive behavior was typical of Sirica. He was a little man, a heretofore nondescript member of the judiciary, who loved the limelight which, like rain, fell upon the fair-minded and prejudiced alike. Reviewing a transcript of the trial, redacting identities, and recognizing the grab for fame, any first-year law student would recognize in Sirica a judge who might as well have been seated with the prosecution team.

In the Senate hearing with Sam Ervin as the Chairman of the Watergate Committee, Al was questioned by Senator Lowell Weicker. Each person who testified before that committee was questioned by the senator from his home state and was once again forced to tell his story in excruciating detail. In preparing for this testimony, Al had met previously with the senator and his staff at Weicker's home in Greenwich, Connecticut.

Alfred Baldwin's testimony is recorded for history in the publication of the Final Report from the Senate and House Judiciary Committees.

14

ENCOUNTERS IN THE WITNESS ROOM

Baldwin encountered some of the players in the Watergate saga in the witness rooms where those who were to give testimony in the various trials and investigations gathered.

One person he wanted to talk to was Carl Shoffler, one of the arresting officers of the D.C. police department. Shoffler was one of the officers Baldwin saw on the balcony of Democratic National Headquarters the morning of June 17. In conversation with Shoffler, the lawman acknowledged making eye contact with Al across the avenue between the Watergate complex and HoJo's. He also remembered seeing Al on the grounds of the Washington Monument at the time of the demonstrations. Shoffler was a man to be admired, and he and Baldwin became friends.

Paul Leeper was the senior officer of the threesome that had arrested the burglars which included Shoffler and John Barrett. Barrett, according to Baldwin, has milked his Watergate role. He shows up at any Watergate program, anniversary, or event. He is always in the audience and always comes up to the microphone and always has something to add. Over the years, he has continuously expanded his first-hand knowledge of the scandal. On one of the anniversaries, Al thinks it was the 40th, one of the major channels broadcast an interview with Barrett in which he goes into this dissertation of what Al Baldwin did, what Al Baldwin saw. As he had no such knowledge, Baldwin confronted him about it.

Al related *I encountered James McCord during the criminal trial of January 1973. It just so happened that this turned out to be the final face-to-face meeting I had with him. As we shook hands he said, "Stay safe," and I replied, "Same, James." I noted the words enough to mention them to my attorney.*

During one of the trials, Baldwin was told that an article had come out in the magazine *Esquire* in which Frank Sturgis (aka Frank Fiorini) revealed that he had a contract to kill a Cuban woman in New York and that Al Baldwin of Connecticut was his second target. For some reason he had never been able to fulfill the first mission, so he never went on to the second and so by some stroke of luck, he did not come looking for Baldwin. Naturally, Al was bothered, and when he had the opportunity, he approached Sturgis while the two men were sequestered in the witness room. The hit man's answer was: "Don't take it personally—it was strictly business."

The night Baldwin and McCord circled McGovern Headquarters, Frank Sturgis was the man who got in the back seat of McCord's car. Later, Al told McCord, *"You know, Frank Sturgis bothers me—he is dangerous—he's a dangerous man," and McCord said, "Yes," and I said, "There's something about him—I can't put my finger on it but man I'm going to avoid him and I'm going to make sure that what I say in front of him."*

Everything about Sturgis' background could only have strengthened that opinion. It was said that he was to assassinate Fidel Castro using a ring containing poison. He was a pilot who transported weapons for the CIA. He was a soldier of fortune.

One of the last questions put to Alfred Baldwin by Senator Lowell Weicker as part of the Senate Watergate Committee's investigation, was regarding the accusation that Baldwin was a double agent actually working for the Democrats. One of the sources of what Baldwin claimed was a false allegation was the talk among the witnesses that the only way he, Baldwin, could have avoided prosecution was that he was protected as a mole for the other party. Additional fodder for the rumors were (1) that Martha Mitchell had given out that Baldwin had stated to her that he was a Democrat and (2) that while working as an assistant to James McCord, Baldwin was dating a woman who was employed by a connection to the Democrat National Committee.

The charge that he had been, in 1972, a plant of the Democrats was reignited when Baldwin was later employed as an Assistant Prosecutor under Democrat States Attorney John M. Bailey in Hartford. This Bailey was a son of the Bailey who had been the National Committee Chairman before Larry O'Brien, the one claimed as an uncle when Baldwin successfully sought a tour of the party's headquarters in Washington.

15

YEARS UNDER THE PAUL O'BRIEN CURSE

With testimony behind me, I was not free of Watergate repercussions. Whether engineered by some embittered Republican faction threatened by the CRP's Attorney Paul O'Brien or simply as a result of a reputation destroyed by association with the scandal of the century, I spent years scrounging for a living, unable to find a decent job.

Eventually, I filed a federal lawsuit suing the Committee to Re-elect the President based on various counts. We won the federal trial. There was an award of money which essentially paid off my Washington lawyers. Every time I appeared in the District, I had to have representation by a Washington attorney along with my Connecticut lawyers. My good friend Bob Mirto handled the entire affair pro bono. Both he and the treacherous John Cassidento had devoted many legal hours in my defense.

Interestingly enough, I think I am the only individual who's ever been removed from the Society of Former Special Agents by a legal process. They have a process in considering the removal of an agent. Tom Dodd, who was a former agent, did something with campaign funds when he was a senator *from Connecticut that resulted in a hearing, but the vote was not to remove. In my case, the hearing was scheduled, I believe either in Alaska or Hawaii, at a time when Paul O'Brien's threat that I would never get another job was proving true. Bob Mirto sent a formal letter to the effect that attending the hearing at the scheduled time would prove an undue hardship on me, but it was ignored.*

By 1976, I had circulated my resume widely and had undergone over forty corporate interviews to no avail. Once, having survived the winnowing process to the point where I was to fly to Switzerland for a final assessment by a security firm, I was notified at the airport not to bother.

Finally, I was hired as a substitute teacher by the Superintendent of Public Schools of New Haven, Connecticut, named Barbarito. The next day the local newspaper headline read "Watergate Burglar Hired as a Substitute Teacher." Forced to retract or face a libel suit, the newspaper did retract in small print on page 3 or 4.

In order to pursue a career in education, I pursued a master's degree in education at Southern State University of Connecticut. With credit allowed for college courses already taken, I only had to take a few courses like "Music in the Classroom," and "Art in the Classroom," to be awarded the degree. At that time in Connecticut, a law degree was not considered a doctorate although shortly before I stopped teaching, the State Legislature did deem it to be juris doctorate retroactive to my class of 1963. For some years in addition to teaching at the city level—New Haven—I was an adjunct professor at the Southern State University of Connecticut.

There came a time that I became infected with the ambition to become a prosecutor in the State attorney's office.

I had never taken the bar exam although buried in Watergate litera-ture is the allegation that I tried several times and failed. Almost a quarter of a century after law school, I did take the exam and through some miracle passed on the first attempt.

My name was submitted to the Judicial Commission in Connecticut by John Connelly, then the State Attorney in Waterbury, Connecticut. I received my appointment to the position of Assistant State Attorney, Division of Criminal Justice. I served in the Waterbury State's attorney office for approximately two years.

I was contacted by Jack Bailey, the State Attorney in the Hartford courthouse, and he wanted to know if I wanted to transfer to Hartford. I had developed a reputation as a trial attorney, and he had an open position. Connelly had no objection and encouraged me to make the move since the Hartford office had a reputation regarding appointment to open judgeships. I had no intention of becoming a judge, nevertheless I accepted Bailey's invitation.

My move to Hartford was front page news. Some articles reported that the new job was "pay off" for Watergate. The conspiracy theorists dug up the old accusation that I was a double agent. The basis for these allegations centered around the fact that Jack Bailey was the son of John Bailey, former Democratic National Chairman prior to Larry O'Brien. This is the same John Bailey that I claimed was my uncle in order to obtain a tour of the Watergate Democratic offices days before the break-in. In addition to the local and national media coverage on my move to Hartford, authors of later Watergate books pointed to my employment by a Democrat as anything but normal. Bailey vehemently denied any such connection asserting that his decision was based on my trial record. He later justified the hiring by saying, "He had the FBI background, so he communicates well with police. He's been an inner-city teacher. He's personable, he deserved the chance."

It took several years for the Watergate notoriety to abate. I remained with the Hartford office up to my retirement in the late 1990s.

In an article in the *Hartford Courant* some twenty-five years after Watergate, Al Baldwin was described as "a candid, rough and tumble, street-smart prosecutor." A defense attorney said, "Al tells you what he's thinking, you get what you see." His boss, Chief State's Attorney John M.

Bailey, was quoted as saying, "He doesn't suffer fools lightly, but overall he's been an excellent prosecutor."

As an example of the strange twists that happened in life, just prior to my retirement from the states attorney's office, FBI agent Daniel Mayham, one of the team along with Angelo Lanno who interrogated me after I agreed to cooperate with the Watergate prosecution, was assigned to the Hartford FBI office. Learning of my presence, he called to invite me to his retirement dinner from the Bureau. I had a conflict and could not attend. The night of the affair, there was a heavy snowstorm. There's a section of Hartford where you have to drive over this semi-mountain and negotiate a steep decline. Mayham, full of plans for the next stage of his life, lost control of his car. Tragically, he was killed, and his son was seriously injured.

16

THE PUZZLE PUT TOGETHER

In law, a substantial amount of circumstantial evidence can be as compelling as direct evidence. Al Baldwin is convinced that the pieces of the puzzle added by the candid account of his personal experience of working with James McCord during those critical weeks of 1972 has provided sufficient circumstantial evidence that, coupled with the direct evidence, allows the historian to finally answer the question "WHY WATERGATE?"

The literature of Watergate is vast. Participants, observers, revisionists, conspiracy theorists, revanchists have all written their books and articles and produced their television specials. Many of these accounts have advanced the notion that Richard Nixon was a key player in the Watergate phenomena. The evidence clearly establishes that rather than being an instigator, he was the reason for Watergate.

Nixon distrusted the intelligence community and was dissatisfied with their performance. For example, the famous Plumbers at the center of Watergate were recruited because the intelligence people could not identify the source of the leaks of confidential information at the highest level in

Washington. Nixon's ire was especially aroused by Richard Helms and the CIA. One reason for his animosity was Helms' refusal to allow the agency to be used for political purposes.

Early in his presidency, Nixon attempted to remove Helms but failed. His next move was to distance himself from the CIA chief by banning him from the prestigious inner circle at the White House. Rather than report directly to the nation's chief executive, Helms was downgraded to reporting to the Secretary of State, Henry Kissinger. Finally, Richard Helms was removed from the Washington scene. He was replaced as CIA director and appointed ambassador to Iran.

Like Smiley and his allies in John LaCarre's "Circus," the British intelligence agency, the old hands at the CIA might have been marginalized by Nixon's cutting them from the mainstream of power, but they continued to be loyal to the patriotic mission of protecting the country with the valuable weapon of <u>information</u>. And they still possessed the skills of their trade like George Smiley who has been described as masking his inner cunning, mastering the tradecraft of spying, and allowing his adversaries to underestimate him to achieve his goals.

In a review of the odd details, the inexplicable episodes, and the conflicting evidence that appears all along the arc of events known as "Watergate," pieces of the puzzle that make up the emerging picture of truth inserted in the record by Al Baldwin in his account presents the circumstantial evidence that supports the claim that the why of Watergate was the removal of a president.

Outlined In the following pages are the various puzzle pieces that form the circumstantial evidence that the Why? of the Watergate burglary was to crack the door that would lead inevitably to the cornered President Richard Nixon's recognition that his only choice was to resign facing as he was the certainty of removal by successful impeachment:

Puzzle piece 1: Why was Alfred Baldwin plucked from New England and recruited as James McCord's assistant in charge of security at the Committee to Re-elect the President?

A. Of all the names on the list of former FBI agents, why Alfred Baldwin in New England and not an available agent in Washington, D.C.?

B. Why the urgency? Interview next day after initial contact? Covert transportation?

Puzzle piece 2: Why the out-of-ordinary decision-to-employ process?

A. McCord did not conduct anything like a traditional interview. Did not ask for basic information like education, deployment as Marine, locations of FBI service, or references even though the job would put him in company with VIPs and require that he carry a gun.

B. Fred LaRue's main concern: was Baldwin ready to travel?

C. No formal employment application when such documentation is required for even entry-level, minimum wage positions

Puzzle piece 3: Why retain Baldwin at the Committee to Re-elect even though his performance had not been stellar?

A. Martha Mitchell's complaints although excused as coming from a troubled person were still not a positive

B. The statement Baldwin made to the press in Michigan as to the actions of the President of the United States violated the most basic tenant of security protocol

C. Baldwin's relationship with a secretary from a known Democrat law firm

Explanation: Not only had Alfred Baldwin been thoroughly vetted by the CIA, he had a role to play of which he was unaware

Puzzle piece 4: The indoctrination of Alfred Baldwin

A. The Lafayette Square conversation revealing McCord's poor opinion of the performance and integrity of Nixon and his men an opening salvo.

B. McCord's lack of respect for Liddy and Hunt made clear to Baldwin on more than one occasion

C. After-dinner conversations at the McCord home made of Baldwin a confidante

D. McCord's interest in removing a president revealed to Baldwin without the latter's expressing loyalty to the President

E. Revelations of McCord's connections with WWII intelligence community including the OSS played to Baldwin's family background i.e. father's WWI service, uncle's WWII service.

F. McCord planted information about his connections to Allan Dulles and Richard Helms, the FBI and the CIA over the hours Baldwin was his audience when the two men were together in the room at Howard Johnson's monitoring the telephone at the DNC

G. McCord planted his objections to Nixon's rapport with China based on some 50 disappeared intelligence connections in deal with Russia.

H. It was Baldwin's second-hand knowledge of Mitchell's connection to the unlawful campaign tactics of Gemstone revealed to him by James McCord that put Mitchell's friend Nixon in the crosshairs and it was Baldwin's lawyer Cassidento who gave the DNC the advantage of knowing what Baldwin would testify even before Baldwin agreed to testify.

Explanation: James McCord scripted Alfred Baldwin to cooperate with the government knowing that is what he would do

Puzzle piece 5: Puzzling phenomena that became understandable after the fact:

A. Business card with magic telephone number that allowed Baldwin to carry weapon on airplane, could be used as a get out of jail free card, accommodated breaches of security like that of getting close to AirForce1 at Andrews which hinted McCord still connected to intelligence state.

B. McCord's sending Baldwin back to Connecticut for his personal vehicle which provided transport for him after the break-in.

Puzzle piece 6: Puzzling behavior anticipating apprehension in midst of break-in.

A. Baldwin's tour of Democrat National Headquarters ostensibly to locate Lawrence O'Brien's office which surely McCord already knew. Baldwin determined O'Brien would not be back in the office until after the Miami convention so what need was there to fix the bug that was not transmitting?

B. In spite of long delay occasioned by a worker staying late in Democrat National Headquarters, McCord held out to break in that night, June 16, 1972.

C. McCord called the shots, not Liddy

D. McCord's insistence on placing tape on Watergate door himself, the amateur placement of tape, McCord's lying that he had removed it

E. McCord removed all personal items of identification from his person in HoJo room

F. McCord's last-minute and brief instructions to Baldwin re walkie-talkie yet he had fellow burglars silence the radio preventing Baldwin's alert from warning the culprits.

Puzzle piece 7: Conversations both via telephone and person to person, plus one letter between McCord and Baldwin after the cover-up is publicly uncovered and trials and hearings are in process

   A. Every contact included the phrases from McCord to Baldwin: "Al, do what you have to do" and "don't hold back."

   B. In many conversations McCord added, "You need to tell the truth. I have no problem with what you are going to do."

   C. In a letter to Baldwin from McCord dated February 16, 1975, McCord writes: "The nation of course owes you a debt for what you did, and for your own integrity."

E. PUZZLING FACTS NEVER EXPLAINED

   1. A key to Ida Maxine Wells' desk was found in the pocket of burglar Eugenio Martinez. In 2016, it was revealed that Martinez was on the CIA payroll at the time of the break-in.
   2. The presence just down the street from Watergate of the three *off-duty* arresting officers. Al Baldwin has said that everyone involved in the Watergate break-in had intelligence

backgrounds including Carl Schoffler. Despite Schoffler's continued denials, were the police alerted as to the break-in?

Statement of Alfred Baldwin:

After years of contemplation of what I observed as a participant in the events that have become part of our history as one of the country's most far-reaching political scandals, I have written this account. I have been as honest and forthright as documentation I had saved and my memory allowed.

I believe the only logical conclusion one can reach after evaluating this account is that Watergate was a well-planned operation orchestrated by certain individuals with intelligence backgrounds and having access to the facilities necessary to plan and execute the enterprise of removing a deeply flawed president from office.

Not only was James McCord one of those individuals, I have no doubt that Richard Helms was another. Even though Allen Dulles died in 1968, I truly believe he was also involved. Those in the CIA who distrusted Richard Nixon would have watched with trepidation his political comeback after back-to-back losses for the presidency in 1960 and then for governor of California in 1962. Nixon's success as he moved toward and gained the White House in 1968 would have aroused alarm among those at the CIA who had inside knowledge of the machinations of the former vice president.

APPENDIX

The letter

7 Winder Court
Rockville Md 20850
February 15, 1975
Dear Al,

I am writing in regard to a handful of questions, the results of which may make a world of difference in my current case which is now on appeal. In asking the questions, I am seeking only the truth and nothing more and I knew that you would tell the truth. Here are the questions:

1. How much did Silbert[5]and the other prosecutors learn of any conversation with O'Brady on July 3rd, 1972, when I told him about John Mitchell and the other facets of Watergate? I would have assumed that practically everything I told O'Grady[6] would have been relayed to them; I am sure under

---

5 Earl Silbert, Chief Prosecutor; Assistant U. S. Attorney for the District of Columbia
6 J. Terrence O'Grady Washington Attorney for Alfred Baldwin

the circumstances I would have done so had I been in your shoes. So the question is how much did you tell them, and how much went through your attorneys.

2. How much of what I told O'Grady went to the FBI? You have testified that you began cooperating with the FBI on June 25, 1972, so I assumed that everything I told O'Grady went directly to them immediately, if you were working with them at the time. Is that correct? (Paul O'Brien has said that you were "under complete FBI control" as of June 25, working as an informant for them.)

3. Glanzer[7] said to me in April 1973 that my conversation with you on July 3, 1972, was wiretapped at the time. Is this correct and at whose instructions? Did Glanzer and Silbert receive the results of the wiretapping?

4. Are there other indications learned by you during the summer and fall that the government was wiretapping my telephone conversations elsewhere, at home, at my office, and elsewhere, reporting such conversations as wiretapping "take," or under a confidential source of memoranda?

5. What is the true story of the Parkinson[8] "take the fifth" story?

6. What is the true story on the press story transcription of early 1973 just before trial (the *Los Angeles Times* transcript made by the prosecutors) in which they erroneously quoted you as saying that the operation was a "CIA" operation, instead of a "CRP" operation? Who made the transcript, Silbert or Glanzer?

I am sure you can see the immediate relevance of the answers to the above questions to my Supreme Court appeal. If you have any questions

---

7 Seymour Glanzer, Assistant U. S. Attorney
8 Kenneth Parkinson, Attorney for the Committee to Re-elect the President

or would find it easier to answer the questions by telephone rather than in writing, you can call me at 301/762-5032 collect. If you prefer to write you can simply write the answers on the back of the copy of the letter if you want. All I am seeking is the information, in whatever form it is easiest for you to provide it.

I will always regret the wrong I did to you in bringing you into this whole matter. I knew that it has been as difficult for you as for us, perhaps in many ways moreso. I have always been glad that you took the course which you did and that you undertook to tell the truth as you knew it. I tried to correct with Sirica in my March 1973 letter some mistaken impressions he received from your testimony, and I believe I was successful in that effort. The nation, of course, owes you a debt for what you did and for your own integrity. I hope in time, when I am able, to be able to make it up to you as well.

Our family all sends their best. Thank you.
Signed
Jim McCord

AUTHOR'S POSTSCRIPT

I signed a contract with Media Arts based in Vero Beach, Florida, to conduct a series of videotaped interviews with Alfred Carlton Baldwin III and to use that record as the basis for a book about his involvement in what would become known around the world as "Watergate." Over the course of several months of 2018 in Media Arts' studio, he told me the story of the part he played in the Watergate political events of 1972. The result is this book, The *Puzzle of Watergate*, which has not, I am obliged to point out, has not been finally authorized by Mr. Baldwin.

My interest in the project of making a record of Al's experience went beyond a paying job. I had been a Goldwater Young Republican. I watched the destruction of the president with a sore heart because I had worked side by side with Nixon supporters who worked for his election and reelection. I know it is hokey, but to a man each of our group loved her country. It was a time of great upheaval with wave after wave of attacks in the form of marches and protests, invasions of citadels of government and education, and betraying state secrets to applause. We supported change—we wanted to destroy Jim Crow that had been protected by the Democrats for a hundred years. We wanted forthrightness in our leadership. We wanted change—but not chaos.

I had read a great deal of the Watergate literature and approached about the job of telling Baldwin's story, I felt here was a chance for me to be part of adding to the conglomerate tale that was the sum of all the accounts of the participants. The Watergate Seven, all dead save Liddy, had all told their stories individually. Baldwin, the eighth man, the listener, who was one of a handful of people who knew what the people said on the covertly tapped telephone at Democrat Headquarters, who had been the lookout for the burglars, who was the first to cooperate with the government, who was the one person there the night of the break-in who had not written a book, interested me. I am a believer in what Churchill called "the flickering light of history" and I felt it would be a privilege to bring whatever Al Baldwin could add out of the shadows for the upcoming 50th anniversary of the Watergate break-in—June 17, 2022.[9]

Hence, I had agreed to do the job. I found Al Baldwin likeable but not the stuff of heroes.

Baldwin's native state is Connecticut and I know nothing about his reputation there, but after he spent the winter in Vero for some years, he left behind a reputation that does not encourage any further connection. Over those months of our collaboration, he quarreled with and was evicted by a sequence of landlords. At the last place he resided, an assisted living facility, he complained constantly to the management and even threatened, citing his legal background, to shut down the place if they did not comply with his demands.

I acknowledge that he has terminal cancer and was undergoing treatment over that same duration and such an ordeal can change a person's behavior. I know that he has enjoyed the friendship of honorable and reputable men in public life. To this day, the friend of his youth, Robert Mirto, continues to champion his cause.

Over the months of our sessions when I videoed our interviews, his irascibility was never directed toward me. However, there would sometimes

---

9 Baldwin specifically exonerated Maureen Dean of any involvement which should forever lay to rest any doubts on that score. I have to say that in 1973 I and many other Republicans of my acquaintance found John Dean's disloyalty reprehensible.

niggle, perhaps in my reptilian brain, a warning that the parts of his presented self did not jibe.

In writing his story and mulling the contradictions in his character that I perceived, my take on Al Baldwin is this: He aspires to be, and sees himself as the dominant male, but this self-image often turns him into a bully when a plan is thwarted or his comfort threatened.

Al's father believed that a lie was a source of evil and he drilled the importance of truth into the son. As Al emphasizes several times in his story, he learned the lesson well and contends that he cannot abide a liar. On the tape, he says that when he discovers a man is a liar, he puts him out of his life. But there is a great contradiction between that stated conviction and the ease with which Al Baldwin can don a role that is a complete lie.

When he was in law enforcement, telling the truth was often not an option. Intelligence gathering and interrogation tactics sometimes call for misrepresentation. The job requires subterfuge. The alias and the lie are standard in an operative's tradecraft.

But by the time Baldwin inserted himself among the anti-war protests of the '70s as an undercover operative, had he forgotten the feel of truth? He often used an alias, could not tell a girlfriend his true identity, introduced himself as Bill Johnson to fool unsuspecting secretaries. Can the line between the truth and the lie be maintained in any spook's life?

Although Baldwin was an FBI agent for only three years, and over a half century had gone by since he was an active law enforcement officer, he still produced his FBI badge when seeking privilege in Vero Beach. In his account of his undercover work, he says he produced his Marine officer's ID when confronted by a military man. I daresay he still did that in Vero when he thought it would be advantageous though he had not been in the Corps for some sixty years and his Corps career only lasted from 1957 to 1960. People who routinely misuse current or past status to get something, or get it faster, are not uncommon, but this is not the behavior of a man of integrity.

Al believes he was chosen by James McCord, a man distinguished in intelligence circles, as an assistant because a CIA profile indicated he was the man for the job. Did that profile draw a picture of a trustworthy patriot? A dilettante who went from a short term in the Marines to a short term at the FBI to a short-term marriage to a woman he did not know had connections to the mob? Did McCord choose Baldwin because he, McCord, knew that he, Baldwin, would tell the truth or because he, Baldwin, would tell all he had been primed to tell? And that "all" McCord made sure would include a directional arrow to John Mitchell which would turn right into the White House? Did Baldwin's profile indicate trustworthiness was not his strong suit? In McCord's letter included as an attachment in this book, did McCord call his sidekick a "patriot" with tongue-in-cheek?

Baldwin asserts that James McCord would not lie about the CIA's involvement in the Watergate break-in. But is it not naive to deny that a CIA loyalist by training and instinct would do so?

None of his possible character flaws means that Al Baldwin is not telling the truth about what he saw and heard over May and June of 1972. For what it adds to the wheels within wheels of Watergate history is for the Watergate experts to determine. I did fact-checking using available public services as far as they would take me but some of the events and actors in the events were beyond that purview.

All I can say is that this account is what Alfred Baldwin told me.

THE END